Wise Lord
of the Sky

Wise Lord of the Sky

PERSIAN MYTH

MYTH AND MANKIND

WISE LORD OF THE SKY: Persian Myth

Writers: Tony Allan (The Epic of the Kings, Land of the Story-Tellers, The Persian Legacy), Charles Phillips (The Persian World, The Flames of Wisdom), Michael Kerrigan (Legends of the Early World)
Consultant: Dr Vesta Sarkhosh Curtis

Created, edited and designed by
Duncan Baird Publishers
Castle House
75–76 Wells Street
London W1P 3RE

DUNCAN BAIRD PUBLISHERS
Managing Editor: Diana Loxley
Managing Art Editor: Clare Thorpe
Series Editor: Christopher Westhorp
Editor: Mark McDowall
Designers: Gail Jones, Clare Thorpe
Picture Researcher: Cecilia Weston-Baker
Commissioned Illustrations: Jo Donegan
Map Artwork: Lorraine Harrison
Artwork Borders: Iona McGlashan
Editorial Researcher: Clifford Bishop

TIME-LIFE BOOKS
Time-Life INC. President and CEO: George Artandi
Time-Life International President: Stephen R. Frary

Staff for WISE LORD OF THE SKY: Persian Myth
Editorial Manager: Tony Allan
Design Consultant: Mary Staples
Editorial Production: Ruth Vos

Published by Time-Life Books BV, Amsterdam
First Time-Life English language printing 1999
TIME-LIFE is a trademark of
Time Warner Inc, USA

ISBN 0 7054 3633 0

Colour separation by Colourscan, Singapore
Printed and bound by Milanostampa, SpA, Farigliano, Italy

Title page: The Persian king Khusrow I and his courtiers try to deduce the rules of chess, from a 16th-century illustrated manuscript of Firdowsi's *Shahnameh*.

Contents page: A Sasanian bronze statuette of a mounted rider, *c.*5th century AD.

30 29 28 27 26 25 24 23 22 21 20 19 18 17 16 15 14 13 12 11 10 9 8 7 6 5 4 3 2

Contents

THE PERSIAN WORLD

In about 500BC Darius the Great, self-styled "King of Kings" and ruler of the vast Persian empire, began work on a magnificent new capital city at Persepolis on the Marv Dasht plain in southern Iran. When completed, its great palace contained an *apadana*, or audience hall, capable of holding 10,000 people – and here, on a golden throne, the Persian monarch received tribute each year from his subjects. And for the many centuries since classical writers such as Herodotus (*c.*485–425BC) described this land of the Orient, this is the image that Persia has conjured for the Western world – a vivid picture of a land of romance ruled by powerful kings possessed of immeasurable wealth, a land of stark deserts, shaded gardens and glittering palaces.

The word "Persia" began life as the name of a nomadic tribe. It was called the Parsa, and came from Parsuash or Parsumash. The Parsa formed one part of an influx of Aryan nomads from the steppes of Asia who swept onto the plateau of Iran sometime during the latter part of the second millennium BC. It was a time of vast migrations when other tribes also settled in Iran, notably the Medes who were to found a great Iranian empire. Scholars still argue about when these people crossed Iran and where exactly they came to rest, but it is clear that they arrived on the plateau from the northeast and moved westwards, fanning out in all directions when they reached the Zagros Mountains of western Iran. By 1000BC, according to one theory, the nomads had crossed the entire plateau, with some tribes doubtless settling on the way, and their first appearance in eastern Iran might therefore be placed decades or even centuries earlier.

Iranians have long preferred to call their country Iran ("Land of the Aryans") rather than Persia, a name to which the West clung for its romantic associations, and in 1934 the Tehran government officially changed the name of the nation. Yet the Aryans did not create the country: archaeological evidence shows that the Iranian plateau had a developed civilization millennia before the steppe nomads began their migrations. The Medes and Persians formed the greatest empires the world had yet seen, building on ancient foundations as well as on the strength they had developed in their own nomadic past. Yet they also take their place among the many racial groups both before and since who have swept into Iran, transforming and being transformed by this great country.

Opposite: **Court dignitaries ascend a staircase in the palace of Darius at Persepolis, *c.*6th century BC.**

Below: **Lustreware in the form of a *mihrab* – a prayer niche which indicates the direction of Mecca. Kashan, central Persia, *c.*14th century.**

Empires of the Sand

Unlike the rich and fertile land that produced the early Mesopotamian civilizations, the plains of central Persia were unforgiving deserts. But amid the vast expanse of territory that spread eastwards from the banks of the Tigris countless kingdoms continued to struggle for supremacy until the triumphant dawn of the Muslim age.

Iran lies on a plateau sandwiched between two expanses of salt water: the Caspian Sea to the north and the Persian Gulf to the south. And with almost all of the country more than 450 metres above sea level and one-third of it either towering mountain or windswept desert, water has always been the key to survival on the inhospitable plains.

To the west of these lands tower the Zagros Mountains beyond which lies the fertile plain watered by the Tigris and Euphrates rivers where the civilizations of Sumer, Babylon and Assyria flourished. To the north, by the southerly shores of the Caspian Sea, runs another imposing range, the Alburz Mountains which boast the highest peak in Iran, Mount Demavand.

At the eastern edge of this range, the mountains fall away into the low hills and steppes of Khorasan, which travellers found easy to traverse. Over the centuries they became established as a gateway to Iran from Turkmenistan and the Central Asian plains, through which wave after wave of nomads and warriors swept – including in the late second millennium BC the Medes and Persians.

In the southeast corner of the Mesopotamian plain, as the countryside runs down from the Zagros to the shores of the Persian Gulf, is the lush region now known as Khuzistan, which was home to the Iranian civilization of Elam (see page 10). But little flourished in Persia's sun-baked deserts.

The World's First Farmers

Geologists have shown, however, that for vast lengths of prehistoric time much of the Iranian plateau was an inland freshwater lake. Modern humans, who spread through the world from around 35,000BC, lived as hunters and gatherers high on the mountainsides – for even the mountain valleys were flooded. Then, sometime before 10,000BC, the water level began to fall as rains dried up following a more general climate change. As the waters retreated, people came down into lower lands. At first they followed the animals that they hunted, but from about 9000BC in Iran and throughout the Middle East these hardy hunters began to experiment with a more settled way of

Animals influenced many aspects of early human culture, the bull being particularly associated with strength and fertility. This ancient clay vessel is from Amlash, in northwestern Iran.

life, making the first tentative steps in domesticating plants and animals. By 6000BC there were many farming villages on the Iranian plateau.

At Siyalk, south of Tehran, archaeologists have uncovered evidence of a settlement dating from the early fifth millennium BC. The people of Siyalk lived in houses made of branches, wore necklaces of shells, painted their pots in patterns thought by historians to be an imitation of basket-work, and carved pictures of animals and humans in bone used for the handles of implements. They had moved beyond subsistence and were able to create a surplus with which to trade. Among the shells they wore were some only found 950 kilometres away on the shores of the Persian Gulf.

In time these people learned to build more permanent mud-brick dwellings; they developed the potter's wheel and the kiln and they learned to make tools from metal, including the plough. Farming thus became more sophisticated and trade naturally flourished, notably in foods: in the early fourth millennium BC wheat and barley, which grow wild in Iran, first appeared in Europe and Egypt as a result of long-distance commerce.

Successive Persian princes fought for supremacy in the land that stretched eastwards from Mesopotamia towards Afghanistan, shifting the boundaries of the land we know as Persia. The key cities, rivers and regions are marked on the map below.

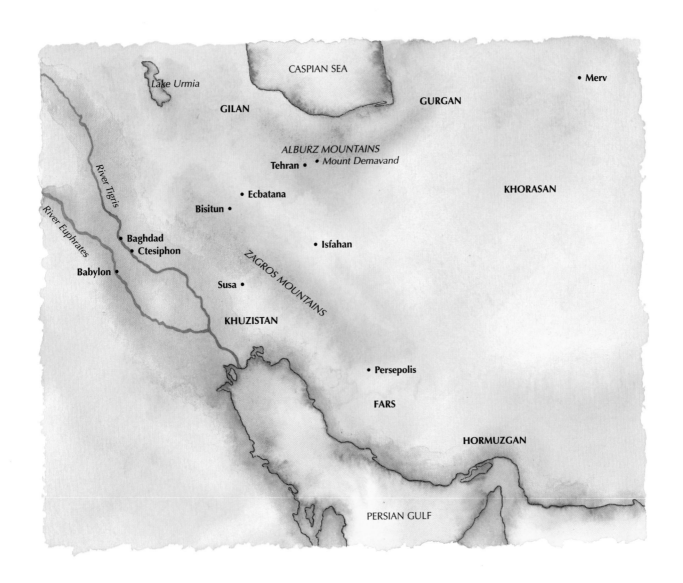

A Great Leap Forwards

From the late fourth millennium BC the peoples of Mesopotamia began to gather in larger settlements, creating what scholars believe was the world's oldest urban civilization at Sumer. But on the Iranian plateau life could only flourish where there was water, and people continued to live in small, isolated oases. However, at the start of the third millennium BC, there emerged on the rich plain of Khuzistan a people who were able to match the urban development of Mesopotamia: the Elamites.

Archaeologists tell us that it was in Sumer and Elam in this era that humankind invented writing. Clay tablets inscribed with a written script and dated to c.3300BC have been uncovered at Uruk, a Sumerian city-state near the Euphrates almost 400 kilometres north of the Persian Gulf, and at Susa in southwestern Iran. They appear to have been merchants' records, detailing sales of crops or cattle. This first written script contained identifiable images of real things such as fish or a human head; each symbol represented an idea or an entire word

Pottery and the Arts

The ancient decorated pots found in Iran are without parallel elsewhere in the region and have led archaeologists to call the culture that produced them in the fifth to fourth millennia BC the "painted pottery civilization".

This Iranian painted clay vase is typical of early Middle Eastern pottery between the 5th and 4th millennia BC.

The inhabitants of the Iranian plain had a special genius for making and decorating clay pots and figures. Theirs was a truly ancient art, for although pottery had first appeared in Japan, c.11,000BC, it was independently developed in the Near East in about 8000BC.

The earliest pots were made by building up pieces or coils of clay. Then, in the early fifth millennium BC, a primitive wheel was devised in the form of a circular slat of wood placed on the ground and turned by an assistant. The first true potter's wheel was developed around 4500BC, and improvements in the design of kilns soon allowed artisans to vary precisely the heat with which they fired their works. By changing the temperature they could alter the pots' colour and produce wares in red, green, rose and grey.

They painted their pieces with lithe, intensely realistic images of serpents, panthers, storks, mouflons (the ancestors of sheep) and other wildlife. They quickly began to produce abstract images of these animals – in which the horns, for instance, were greatly exaggerated for decorative effect or the creatures' bodies were represented by geometric shapes such as a triangle.

The potters also produced clay figurines of animals which were perhaps used as toys or religious offerings to a deity of the fields. Another common representation was that of a naked woman, which some scholars have interpreted as a Great Mother fertility goddess.

rather than a part of a word or a letter. Scribes used a pointed stylus made from a reed to scratch images into the tablets while the clay was soft. The tablets were then laid out to harden in the sun.

Scholars now believe that a similar script which they call "proto-Elamite" was separately developed in neighbouring Elam at around the same time. The two scripts have many of the same number signs but appear to have been written in different languages, the Sumerian and Elamite tongues of the period.

Over the following centuries the scripts became more complex. By *c.*2500BC variants of them were used across the Mesopotamian plain for building dedications and to write down prayers, letters and official records. These scripts were later called "cuneiform", a word that is derived from the Latin *cuneus* ("wedge") and means wedge-shaped, because the scribes made broad, angular impressions with their styluses.

This stone inscription shows cuneiform writing, which would have been read from left to right. It dates from the Akkadian era, *c.*7th century BC.

The Emergence of Elam

The Elamites were a tribe from the southern region of the Zagros Mountains who had established a dynasty in the region of modern Khuzistan by 2700BC. Their kingdom became locked in a close and often violent embrace with the neighbouring city states of Mesopotamia. Elam's power waxed and waned but at one stage spread far into Babylonia and eastwards across the Iranian plateau. The settlement of Anshan, east of the Zagros in southern Iran, was a major Elamite base.

Throughout this period the Elamites, the more northerly Zagros tribes and those of the plateau itself were closely connected to the Mesopotamian city-states by trade as well as by war. Gold, tin, copper and stone from Iran – along with lead and semi-precious stones such as lapis lazuli from further afield – were transported through the passes of the Zagros down to the green lowlands where monarchs keen to demonstrate the glory of their dynasties were ever determined to outdo one another in the grandeur of their temples and palaces.

Around 2300BC a Semitic leader named Sargon of Agade expanded from a base in central Mesopotamia to conquer Sumer and most of the plain, founding the Akkadian dynasty that dominated Elam and ruled until *c.*2279BC. Shortly afterwards Elam won back its independence, but was then conquered by the Guti, another Zagros tribe. In the century either side of 2000BC Sumerian power was reasserted by kings known to scholars as the third dynasty of Ur – and Elam came under their rule. As this dynasty weakened, another Zagros power, the kingdom of Simash, triumphed. It was a recurring pattern: when the pre-eminent Babylonian or Sumerian power began to weaken, the tribesmen of the Zagros would pour down from the mountains to take advantage, only to be repulsed when the kingdoms of the plain had recovered their strength.

If the kings of Zagros were successful in war they ordered victory reliefs to be carved. A significant Iranian rock carving was made for King Annubanini of the Lullubi near the Iranian town of Sar-i Pul-i Zohab: clutching a bow and arrow he stamps on a defeated enemy. Such memorials were strongly influenced by similar carvings made by Mesopotamian kings, notably a celebrated one commissioned by the Akkadian king Naram-Sin (c.2254–2218BC), but they also set a pattern for Iranian rulers – and many a later Iranian monarch commemorated his great prowess on rocks.

From around the nineteenth century BC, Elam came into conflict with the kings of Babylon, a wealthy city on the River Euphrates. The most celebrated of the Babylonian kings of this era, Hammurabi (c.1792–1750BC), won a great empire and decisively defeated Elam in 1764BC. Yet before the century was out, the Elamites had restored their pride under King Kutir-Nahhunte and won a crushing victory over Hammurabi's son, Samsu-iluna (c.1749–1712BC).

After this Elam once again went into decline as the Kassites, another mountain people from the Zagros, took control of Mesopotamia. The Kassite tribe included descendants of a first wave of migrating Aryans from the Asian steppes that had passed through Iran at the beginning of the second millennium BC. As the steppe nomads had migrated, some had settled in the Zagros and some in Mesopotamia. Some had travelled east to India and others had wandered as far as Greece. These peoples were related to the Medes and Persians whose arrival they predated by 500–1,000 years.

The Aryans who had settled in the Zagros mingled with the local tribes and in time established themselves as a warrior class. The Kassites must have been an awesome military force for they held power in the hotbed of Mesopotamia for more than 500 years.

This gold statuette of a man carrying an offering of a goat was found at Susa, in southwest Iran, and dates from c.1150BC, a time of great Elamite success.

The Glory of the Anshanite Dynasty

Elam re-emerged as a great force on the plain after one of its kings, Ige-Halki, founded the Anshanite dynasty in the fourteenth century BC. His grandson Humban-umena (c.1285–1266BC) took the name "Expander of the Empire" and erected a celebrated temple at Liyan on the coast of the Persian Gulf some 400 kilometres to the southeast of the Elamite capital, Susa. His successor Untash-Napirisha (c.1260–1235BC) restored many Elamite temples and cities and built a new capital city for the empire at Chogha Zanbil, forty kilometres southeast of Susa. It contained three palaces and a ziggurat, or stepped temple, that probably once rose to a height of more than fifty metres.

In 1168BC Shatruk-Nahhunte invaded southern Mesopotamia and took back to Susa the Code of Hammurabi, found there by French excavators in the twentieth century. Fourteen years later, a second Kutir-Nahhunte invaded Babylonia and deposed the final Kassite monarch, Enlil-nadin-ahi. For his booty he took the statue of Marduk, the city god of Babylon. Shilhak-Inshushinak (1165–1151BC), who succeeded Kutir-Nahhunte, continued the revival, creating an Elamite empire encompassing the Zagros Mountains, the Tigris valley and land along the Persian Gulf.

But at the height of its glory Elam was toppled. The Babylonian King Nebuchadrezzar I (c.1125–1104BC) defeated the Elamites, looted Susa and returned home with the statue of Marduk. Elam never recovered from this devastating blow. It disappeared altogether from historical records for around 300 years and in later times was never a match for the power of the northern Mesopotamian kingdom of Assyria, which began its rise at the time of Elam's fall and was at its height ruling a vast empire from the ninth to the seventh centuries BC.

The Elamite empire was finally destroyed by the Assyrian king Ashurbanipal, shown here hunting lions from his chariot. This stone relief is from the North Palace at Nineveh, c.640BC.

From c.720BC Elam recovered for a short period, but in 646BC the forces of the Assyrian king Ashurbanipal burst across its borders, sacking Susa and devastating the surrounding lands. By this time, however, a new Iranian power was on the rise: within fifty years the Medes would erupt from their base south of the Caspian Sea to challenge the great powers of Mesopotamia.

The Medes and the Persians

Madai (Medes) and Parsa (Persians) first appear in written history in the Assyrian cuneiform records of King Shalmaneser III (858–824BC). The Persians seem to have come to Iran in the wake of the Medes, and there is evidence that they settled in more than one area: in northwestern Iran near Lake Urmia, in the southwestern Zagros, in territory later called Parsumash, and on the high plains

of Fars in southern Iran, later called Parsa. Both tribes had arrived with the migration of Aryan tribes sometime before 1000BC. At that time they lived peacefully as nomads, hunting and keeping dogs to help them herd cattle, goats and sheep.

Some of these tribesmen served as priests and their rituals included drinking the intoxicating pressed juice of an unidentified plant that was to be known to Zoroastrians as *haoma* and to Indian Aryans as *soma* (see page 35). They worshipped gods and goddesses of fire, water, earth, sky, sun, moon, winds and storm. They also seem to have hailed divinities of a more abstract nature, who represented qualities such as truth, loyalty and courage – as well as amoral, warlike deities whose wrath was to be feared.

In the third millennium BC they learned how to tame the wild horses of the steppes, to build chariots and to make durable weapons – and by the time they began their migrations at least some of them were established as formidable warriors.

The Medes of the Zagros Mountains eventually came together to create a kingdom in northwestern Iran in the seventh century BC. They battled for supremacy with rival tribes until, in 625BC, a Median prince named Cyaxares ousted the fearsome Scythian horsemen who had once seemed unstoppable as they pillaged their way from Assyria to Palestine. Then, in alliance with King Nabopolassar of Babylon, he finally managed to take the Assyrian capital Nineveh in 612BC. The great empire of the Assyrians would never recover.

Cyaxares died in 584BC, leaving an empire that had expanded to encompass lands from western Iran to the River Halys in Asia Minor – an ascendancy that was to be short-lived.

By the time Cyaxares had been succeeded by his son Astyages, a new Iranian power was poised to strike: that of the Persians. In the highland plain of Fars a subject king of the Persian tribe, named Cyrus II, rose up against Astyages. His initial act of defiance was to make a diplomatic pact with the Babylonians, with whom the Medes were now at war; then he engineered an outright revolt in Fars. Cyrus was in fact Astyages's grandson, for the

Persian king's mother was a Median princess who had been married to a Persian king named Cambyses to cement an alliance. The dynasty to which Cyrus belonged was supposedly founded in the seventh century BC by Achaemenes, but this king may not be a historical figure.

Faced with Cyrus's insubordination, Astyages had to assert his supremacy and marched on Fars. On a fateful day in 559BC, many Median troops including a gifted commander named Harpagus defected to the Persian side and Cyrus defeated Astyages. At a stroke the young king won control of the great Median empire for his own Achaemenian dynasty.

In the hour of his first great triumph, Cyrus demonstrated the qualities for which he was to become renowned: tolerance and magnanimity. He treated Astyages respectfully and gave the Medes a privileged position, second only to the Persians, in battle and matters of honour. He set to work consolidating his power on the Iranian plateau, then had to move against Croesus, king of Lydia in Asia Minor, who saw the fall of the Medes as an opportunity to expand his own domain.

Cyrus triumphed over Croesus and then embarked on a military and diplomatic campaign that swelled the empire to an unprecedented size. In Asia Minor his subordinate generals took control of the Greek cities on the coast of the Aegean Sea; and Cyrus himself seems to have extended his territory into the far northeast of Iran.

Next Cyrus seized Babylon, great and heavily fortified city of lore on the Euphrates. On his triumphant entry into the city, in October 539BC, Cyrus approached the statue of the city god Marduk and clasped its hands to indicate that he would accept local customs. And his rule was widely welcomed, not least by the 40,000 Jews who had been held in Babylon since being taken captive by Nebuchadrezzar II in 586BC. Cyrus allowed them to return to Palestine and rebuild the Temple of Solomon there. By victory over Babylon he had won control of its territories in Mesopotamia, Syria and Palestine.

Cyrus's tolerance of Babylonian religion – he even made sacrifices to local gods – was typical of his astute and respectful handling of subject peoples. It was the germ of the legend that grew up

TIMELINE	35,000–2000BC	2000–1000BC

Persia's passage from a land of pagan city-states to a unified Islamic Republic was a long and bloody one. But while the warring kingdoms of the Elamites, Medes and Persians struggled for supremacy, and the Muslim caliphs fought to repel invaders, a great number of striking cultural achievements were made: writing, the art of poetry and an architecture that remains a wonder of the world.

Diorite statue of a king wearing a cap, Sumerian period, c.2000BC.

*c.***35,000BC** Humans spread across Eurasia.
*c.***10,000BC** Climate change dropped the water level and opened up the fertile plains of Persia.
*c.***9000BC** Nomads stalked the Iranian plains.
*c.***6000BC** Farming communities founded.
*c.***3000BC** Beginnings of urbanization under the Sumerians and Elamites. Emergence of writing.
*c.***2300BC** Sargon of Agade founded the Akkadian dynasty.

Above: *Boot-shaped pottery vessel from northwest Iran, c.1000BC.*

*c.***2000BC** Aryan nomads swept onto Iranian plateau. Resurgence of Sumerian power.
*c.***1800BC** Rise of the Babylonian kings.
*c.***1400BC** Rebirth of Elamite power.
*c.***1300BC** Appearance of grey-ware pottery.
*c.***1100BC** Babylonian King Nebuchadrezzar I defeated the Elamites.

around this great king. For freeing the Jews he was hailed in the Old Testament Book of Ezra, where he was cast as the agent of the Lord. In the century after his death he was also the subject of a treatise on the ideal monarch by the Greek historian Xenophon (*c*.435–354BC).

Cyrus's command of his empire was symbolized by his magnificent new capital, Pasargadae ("The Camp of the Persians"), built on the site of his victory over Astyages. But one day he would succumb to defeat. Cyrus met his death in *c*.530BC fighting on the empire's always troublesome northeastern frontier. He left an empire stretching from the Aegean Sea to the River Indus.

Darius the Great

Cyrus's son Cambyses added Egypt to the empire in a campaign between 525 and 522BC, but while he was away a revolt broke out at home. It was led by a man called Gaumata, who claimed to be Bardiyeh, Cyrus's other son who had been murdered. Cambyses marched back to Iran, but he died on the way, probably from an infection.

One of the king's bodyguards, a man called Darius, then travelled with utmost haste to Fars, where with the help of six nobles he killed the false Bardiyeh and took the throne for himself. Darius was said to be a great-grandson of Ariaramnes, one of the grandsons of Achaemenes himself. Whatever the truth of this claim, he was to prove a worthy successor to Cyrus, a man almost his equal in courage and intelligence.

He dedicated the first two years of his reign to combating nineteen separate uprisings that erupted in Persia, Media, Elam and further afield. But two Persian campaigns against the Greek mainland failed: the first, led by Mardonius in 492BC, was abandoned when the Persian fleet was destroyed in a storm; and the second, led by Datis, ended in defeat at the Battle of Marathon in 490BC.

Darius poured his great energy into expanding and consolidating the Achaemenian territories, but also, at home, followed Cyrus in the task of creating palaces and cities worthy of such a vast empire. In southern Iran, near Cyrus's city of Pasargadae, he ordered the construction of a new capital, Persepolis. Here, at the edge of the vast

---

1000–100BC	100BC–AD1000	1000–PRESENT DAY

c.700BC Rise of the Median empire.
c.640BC Assyrians sacked Susa.
625BC Cyaxares ousted Scythians.
612BC Defeat of Assyrian empire.
584BC Death of Cyaxares.
559BC Cyrus the Great defeated the Medes and established the Achaemenian dynasty.
539BC Cyrus seized Babylon.
c.530BC Death of Cyrus.
500BC Darius the Great began work on Persepolis.
490BC Persians defeated by Greeks at the Battle of Marathon.
486BC Death of Darius. His Persian empire fell into slow decline.
331BC Alexander the Great sacked Persepolis.
323BC Death of Alexander.
140BC Mithradates I brings Mesopotamia and western Iran under Parthian rule.

AD224 Ardashir I overpowered the Parthian king Ardavan IV to establish Sasanian dynasty. Zoroastrianism became the official religion.
531 Khusrow I came to power.
610 Khusrow II expanded Sasanian empire into Egypt and Turkey.
620 Byzantine emperor Heraclius killed Khusrow, heralding the decline of Sasanian rule.
632 Death of Mohammed.
633 Bedouin tribesmen invaded Sasanian territory from Arabian deserts.
638 Fall of Sasanian capital, Ctesiphon.
645 Caliphs established their capital at Damascus.
762 Abbasid caliphate moved their capital to Baghdad.
994 Mahmud of Ghazneh ruled eastern Iran.

Left: *Silver and gold bowl with ibexes, Achaemenid period, c.6th century BC.*

1055 Seljuk Turks invaded Persia and established their caliphate.
c.1220 Genghis Khan seized Persia.
1502 Safavid dynasty restored to Iranian rule.
1926 A military coup brought Reza Khan to power.
1934 The Tehran government changed the name of the country to Iran.
1978 Mohammed-Reza Pahlavi deposed by the Islamic Revolution.
1989 Ten million Iranians crowded the streets of Tehran to mourn the death of Ayatollah Khomeini.

Right: *The Shah's peacock throne, now in the Central Bank in Tehran, Qajar period, 1779–1921.*

sumptuous gardens that lay to the northwest of the palace, Darius's tomb was cut into a cliff-face. It overlooked the Achaemenians' magnificent royal road that ran almost 2,700 kilometres from Persepolis to Sardis in Asia Minor and was itself a symbol of the dynasty's glory. Other kings were also buried in the cliff-face, which came to be known as Naqsh-i Rustam.

At Susa, the ancient capital of Elam, Darius had another new palace built, which aimed to celebrate his great achievements. It brought together materials and craftsmen from all corners of his realm: cedar from Lebanon, lapis lazuli from Sogdiana, ivory from Africa, stonemasons from Ionia and carpenters from Egypt.

When Darius died in 486BC he was succeeded by his son Xerxes. The new king led another onslaught on Greece in 480–479BC, capturing Athens and storming the Acropolis. But the adventure ended once again in failure following defeats at the naval battle of Salamis near Athens and at Plataea near Thebes.

Darius ensured that the materials used to build his great palace at Susa reflected the all-encompassing expanse of his empire. This winged bull is composed of glazed bricks which may have been made by Babylonians, c.5th century BC.

After Xerxes's death at the hands of an assassin in 465BC the Achaemenian empire began a slow decline, undermined by a succession of weak monarchs. Nevertheless it survived for a further 150 years, until the final king of the line, Darius III (335–330BC), was ousted by a Macedonian prince known to history as Alexander the Great. The Achaemenian empire, the largest the world had yet seen, left a magnificent legacy in its architectural ruins but also in the example it set by maintaining a remarkably unrepressive imperial rule over such vast territories and so many diverse peoples.

The Rise of Parthian Power

Iranian history took another new direction in the third century BC. By 238BC the ruler of the nomadic Parni tribe, Arsaces, had established a kingdom in the northeastern part of the Iranian plateau. Within 100 years under King Mithradates I, the tribe – now known as Parthians – had taken possession of most of the Mesopotamian plain, forcing the Seleucids (see box opposite) to retreat into Syria.

Parthia's Mithradates II (c.124BC) consolidated the gains and drove back the persistent threat of raiding tribes in the east and also kept at bay the ambitious new power of Rome to the west.

The Parthians grew rich collecting dues from the merchant caravans of the Silk Route that passed directly through their territories on its way from Asia to the Mediterranean. Parthian kings were keen to establish themselves as heirs to the great Iranian dynasties of the past and had "King of Kings", the proud boast of the Achaemenians, engraved on their coinage. Mithradates II had his own triumphant inscription carved on the rockface at Bisitun near that of Darius.

But by the early third century AD Parthian authority on the Iranian plateau was eroding fast. Uprisings and nomadic raids were so common that trade on the Silk Route was abandoned and moved southwards instead through India and thence by sea and land to Rome. In southern Iran Ardashir, king of Fars, began to enlarge his realm at the expense of the surrounding Iranian kingdoms.

Alexander and the Seleucids

After uniting the quarrelling Greek states, Alexander of Macedon took just ten years to forge an empire that stretched from the Aegean to Samarkand. On the way this great general conquered the entire Achaemenian empire, leaving a magnificent legacy for his successors.

Alexander led his 40,000-strong army into Asia Minor in 334BC. The Achaemenian king, Darius III, came to confront the intruder, but was defeated at the Battle of Issus – on the Turkish coast – in November 333. In the struggle Darius lost his treasure and his harem and fled the battlefield.

Alexander next made a detour to Africa, where he conquered Egypt and founded the most celebrated of the many "Alexandrias" that he left in his wake. Back in Asia, a second confrontation with Darius in 331BC at Gaugamela near the River Tigris ended in another victory for the invader. Alexander's exultant troops marched south to Babylon, crossed the Zagros after overcoming the Persians' last stand in a Zagros mountain pass later known as the "Persian Gates" and in 331BC marched into the majestic city of Persepolis.

Here the general must have been deeply impressed by the buildings and luxuries he found, but he ruthlessly broke Persian hearts and any lingering resistance by putting the symbolic heart of the Achaemenian empire to the torch – and allowing his troops to slaughter the soldiers, women and children of the garrison. He made sure that the tomb of Cyrus, one of his own great inspirations as a warrior, was left unharmed but according to some traditions he found and destroyed the *Avesta*, the holy book of the Zoroastrians written in gold on oxhides, which was said to have been hidden near Persepolis.

Darius had fled to northern Iran where later that year he was killed by his own followers; they then tried to proclaim a new king but were defeated by Alexander's troops. Like many a ruler before him on the Iranian plateau, Alexander was then forced to direct his energy to pacifying the northern and eastern fringes of the empire before marching into India where he won a great victory at Hydaspes in

327BC. Four years later he died of fever, aged just thirty-two, in Babylon.

His death sparked a great conflict as his generals fought for corners of his empire. Ptolemy won Egypt; Antigonus, Macedonia; and Seleucus I Nicator ("Conqueror"), the largest portion including Syria, Mesopotamia and most of Persia. After Seleucus's death in 281BC, Iran came under the rule of the Seleucids, named after Seleucus I, the founder of the dynasty. Within fifty years, however, Iranian pride had begun to reassert itself.

The feats of Alexander of Macedon became legendary, fed by the speed with which he reached the Punjab and the fact that he died at the age of just 32. He was feted in many poems and paintings, such as this Mughal miniature which shows the triumphant Alexander entering Persia, *c*.16th century.

Ardashir's conduct was an open affront to the Parthian king, Ardavan (Artabanus IV), and in AD224 on the sundrenched plain of Hormuzgan the two came face to face in single combat. Ardashir killed Ardavan and won both an empire and immortality for his Sasanian dynasty – named after a legendary forbear, Sasan (see page 106).

The Sasanians

Ardashir restored order to the plateau and trade began to move along the Silk Route once more. And with further territorial gains the dynasty acquired wealth and glory.

Zoroastrianism – already a venerable Iranian faith – became the official religion of the empire: the white-robed priests drove the *div* (demons) from the land after the Sasanian armies had won their great victories and Ardashir, associating himself with the great Zoroastrian Wise Lord Ahura Mazda, had an aura of near-divine glory.

As the Parthians had before them, the Sasanians resolutely held Rome at bay. Ardashir's son Shapur (241–272) won a string of resounding victories against the Romans, in 244 defeating and killing Emperor Gordian at Massice (modern Misikhe on the River Euphrates) and then in 259 capturing Emperor Valerian at Edessa in Syria. Shapur had a triumphant relief carved at Naqsh-i-Rustam to commemorate this triumph. Valerian died while a prisoner.

The most celebrated of the dynasty's kings, Khusrow I (531–579), came to the throne in the sixth century. He was a reformer who reorganized and standardized taxes, restricted the powers of great landowners and gave new standing to bureaucratic officers, partly at the expense of the Zoroastrian priesthood. He expanded the empire as far as the Black Sea and moved the court westwards, settling his capital at Ctesiphon. Celebrated as Anushirvan ("He of the Immortal Soul") he is remembered in Iran alongside Cyrus as the epitome of the just ruler. He also reasserted the glory of the dynasty, presiding in his magnificent palace at Ctesiphon over many vast banquets.

His grandson, Khusrow II, led the empire in its last great flourish. By this time the power that was Rome had split into western and eastern halves, with the eastern Byzantine empire ruled from Constantinople (modern Istanbul). In the first two decades of the seventh century Khusrow II led his Sasanian army on a triumphant campaign of expansion into Byzantine territories, capturing Antioch, Damascus, Jerusalem and Sardis as well as Egypt to the south. The Byzantine empire had shrunk to little more than the region around

One of the greatest achievements of the Parthian kings was to keep at bay the ambitious and hitherto unstoppable Roman empire. When the Sasanian king Shapur I defeated and captured Emperor Valerian at Edessa, he commemorated the occasion on a rock-relief at Naqsh-i Rustam, near Persepolis, *c.*AD260.

Constantinople. But within a decade a new Byzantine emperor, Heraclius, took devastating revenge. He marched through Armenia and Azerbaijan onto the Mesopotamian plain and surprised Khusrow II in Ctesiphon. The Byzantine general mounted a siege and fear seemed to madden the city: Khusrow was tracked down in the chamber of his favoured wife, Shirin, and was slain there by his ministers. The dynasty survived, but it was dying – the glorious era of the Sasanians was effectively over.

The Age of Islam

In 636 mounted Bedouin tribesmen swept like a whirlwind out of the deserts of Arabia on the southwestern fringe of the Sasanian territories and in just six years brought the Persian empire to its knees. The Bedouins were little more than desert nomads but they were ruthlessly proficient in a style of raiding warfare which they had practised for years in tribal conflicts and attacks on merchants' caravans. Moreover, they were on fire with the zeal imparted to them by the freshly minted

The ascendancy of Islam in Persia was exemplified by buildings such as the Masjed-e Emam in Isfahan, completed in 1638.

religious faith of Islam, whose founder, the Prophet Mohammed, had died only in 632. They did not fear for their lives in battle, for Islam – which means "submission" – taught them to give up all things to the great God, Allah, and they knew that death while fighting for the faith would send them to heavenly glory.

In 636 at al-Qadisiyya, to the east of the River Euphrates, the Arabs inflicted a devastating defeat on Rustam, great general of the Sasanians. In 638 they overran the great Sasanian capital at Ctesiphon. The king, Yazdagird III, took flight, but was eventually murdered at Merv by a local lord. The Arabs destroyed Sasanian resistance in 642 at the Battle of Nevahand, south of Hamadan.

The ruling caliphs ("deputies") established their capital at Damascus but, with intrigue and assassination marking the line of succession, it was not long before the purity of Islam's beginnings fell away into decadence.

A revolt led by Abu Muslim, a Persian from Khorasan in the northeast, ended with the removal of the Umayyads in 750. They were replaced by the Abbasid caliphs, who in 762 moved their capital to Baghdad – the city on the Tigris that would later become the principal city of Iraq – and actively embraced Persian ways.

As had occurred many times before in the country's history, the people of Iran absorbed and transformed the invaders' way of life: within 200 years of the conquest a new Islamic culture – fusing Arab and Persian influences – was ready to flower (see box opposite). Over the following centuries on the Iranian plateau and further east, various Persian kingdoms rose and fell under the overall control of the Islamic caliphate in Baghdad. In the tenth century under the Samanids there was a flowering of Persian literature culminating in the achievement of the poets Rudaki and Daqiqi. The Samanids' successors, the Ghaznavids, created a great kingdom in modern Afghanistan; Mahmud of Ghazni, who ruled from 994 to 1030, called to his capital the most eminent literary figures of the time, including Firdowsi who created his magnificent epic *Shahnameh* ("Book of Kings") under Mahmud's patronage.

In the eleventh century another band of nomads poured into Iran from the northeast: the warlike Seljuk Turks. They first defeated the Ghaznavids. When they also took Baghdad in 1055 they did not depose the caliph, but their leader Toghrul-beg assumed temporal power as Sultan. In 1200 they were deposed by the bloodthirsty Mongol horde led by Genghis Khan in a devastating onslaught in which two out of every three Iranians are believed to have been slaughtered.

In the sixteenth century the Safavid dynasty, founded in 1502 by Shah Isma'il I, brought the country back under Iranian rule. The most celebrated Safavid ruler, Shah Abbas the Great (1587–1629), was patron of magnificent building works in his capital at Isfahan. After him, however, came further bands of invaders: Afghans, Russians and Turks. But in 1729 the Iranian warlord Nadir Shah once again re-established native control.

The early twentieth century saw a revolution in which army officer Reza Khan seized power. He became shah in 1926, calling himself "King of Kings" in the Achaemenian style. It was his son, Mohammed Reza Shah Pahlavi who, after succeeding his father in September 1941, was deposed in the 1978–79 revolution that created today's Islamic Republic of Iran.

When the religious rule of the republic succeeded the last of the shahs it did not entail a sudden break with the past, for the mullahs resumed control of a land with a venerable religious tradition. Iran after all is a cradle of faiths – scholars believe that the ancient Iranian creed of Zoroastrianism bequeathed significant doctrines to Judaism, Christianity and Islam itself. Today's Iranians, living under strict Islamic rule, look back with swelling pride on their country's long and glorious past. Their birthright is a culture immeasurably rich in the decorative arts and a treasure hoard of stories about gods, prophets, magical intrigues – and the march of great kings to war.

The Flowering of Islam

The collision of Arab and Persian cultures in the years after the conquest had issue in a new amalgam – an Islamic culture that was the glory of the world at the end of the first millennium AD.

The Baghdad caliphs saw the birth of a new Islamic culture; here clerics read the Koran. Persian, *c.*15th century.

A significant aspect of this cultural renaissance was the emergence of an enriched Persian language that was put to delicate use by later poets and chroniclers. Scholars identify three forms of Persian: Old, Middle and Modern.

Old Persian was in use until the third century BC and was one of the languages used for the cuneiform inscriptions of Darius. Middle Persian, or Pahlavi, was the language of the Sasanian empire and was in use up to the ninth century AD. Its successor, Modern Persian, can be traced to the great flowering of Islamic culture about two centuries after the conquest. It contains many Arabic words and is also written in Arabic script. Natives call it Farsi, from the province of Fars, Cyrus's historic homeland.

The first stage in the emergence of a unified Islamic culture came with the flourishing of scholarship in Baghdad. The era of the Sasanians was intensively studied but scholars also embraced learning from all around the world. Historians, poets and philosophers produced work of brilliant originality and enduring influence throughout the tenth and eleventh centuries.

One of the most remarkable achievements of all was that of physician and philosopher Ibn Sina or Avicenna (980–1037), who taught at Isfahan and Hamadan. His pioneering work in medicine was later acclaimed throughout Europe. This influence, though, was not unique, for the achievements of Islamic culture in this era helped to make possible the glories of the European Renaissance four centuries later.

21

ECHOES OF EMPIRE

Cyrus the Great, who reigned from 559 to 529BC, may have achieved eternal fame as the architect of the first great Persian empire, but it was Darius I (521–486BC) who oversaw its finest hours. Under his rule the Achaemenian lands expanded to the Aegean Sea in the west and India in the east. To crown his remarkable achievements he built two of the greatest cities yet seen: in 500BC he began work on his magnificent summer capital at Persepolis, while at Susa he started building his winter headquarters. He made Susa, a once-great Elamite centre, his own by calling together craftsmen and materials from throughout his lands. There was gold from Bactria, lapis lazuli from Sogdiana, turquoise from Egypt and ivory from Ethiopia. And when the city was built, subjects came from all corners of the empire to pay him tribute.

The descendants of Darius added to these foundations until, in 331BC, Alexander put an end to the Achaemenian line. Persepolis was burned and Susa left to the sands of the Khuzestan plain. But today, the ruins of these two sites offer tantalizing glimpses of the ancient Persian kings and still celebrate the glory of Darius the Great.

Above: A limestone relief of a noble from the stairway to the *apadana*, or assembly hall, at Persepolis. The figure reflects Darius's success in dividing his empire into separate satrapies, or administrative zones.

Above: Although Susa survived the worst ravages of Alexander's invasion and remained an important city under the Parthians and Sasanians, little remains of the place today.

Left: The columns of the *apadana* and the palace of Darius gave Persepolis a commanding presence in the plain some 70 kilometres northeast of Shiraz. It was built near Cyrus's capital of Pasargadae.

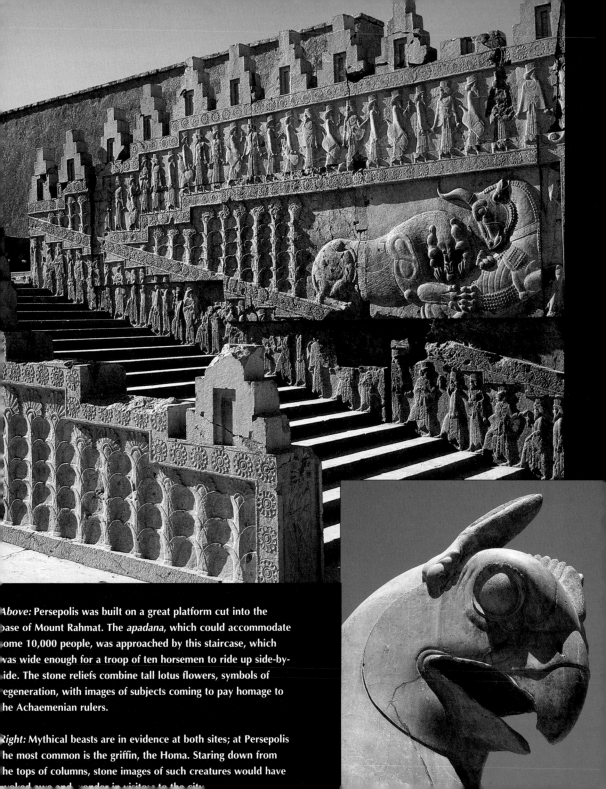

Above: Persepolis was built on a great platform cut into the base of Mount Rahmat. The *apadana*, which could accommodate some 10,000 people, was approached by this staircase, which was wide enough for a troop of ten horsemen to ride up side-by-side. The stone reliefs combine tall lotus flowers, symbols of regeneration, with images of subjects coming to pay homage to the Achaemenian rulers.

Right: Mythical beasts are in evidence at both sites; at Persepolis the most common is the griffin, the Homa. Staring down from the tops of columns, stone images of such creatures would have evoked awe and wonder in visitors to the city.

Above: Darius had an in-depth knowledge of his empire. As a young man he had served under Cyrus in the northeast of Persia and travelled with Cambyses to Egypt (see page 15). Having spent the early years of his reign subduing revolts throughout his lands, he was intimately aware of the cultural diversity his empire embraced. Images like this relief of a Parthian tribute-bearer show how the city was built as a focus for these many disparate peoples.

Right: Although Susa was to become famous as an Achaemenian capital there had been a settlement there since about 4000BC. This bitumen relief of a woman spinning, attended by a servant with a fan, is from neo-Elamite Susa, c.700–600BC, a period which saw the city burned by the Assyrian king Ashurbanipal. The city was in decline from Sasanian times and its ancient heritage was not discovered until British archaeologists explored the site in 1852.

Left: There are more than 3,000 figures carved on walls and staircases at Persepolis, many bearing tribute to the King of Kings. All are shown in great detail, allowing scholars to identify their place of origin. This Lydian delegation is bringing the king fine metal vessels.

Right: Among the finest artifacts discovered at Susa are the polychrome glazed brick reliefs, like this one of an archer of the Persian king's guard, which decorated the palace of Darius. The exotic colouring inside the building, which an ancient inscription credits to craftsmen from Babylonia, was complemented by magnificent terraced gardens outside.

LEGENDS OF THE EARLY WORLD

Thousands of people watched in horror from the hillsides above the city as the royal palace burst into flames. It had taken 200 years to build with the finest materials brought from every corner of the emperor's realms. And in a few hours it was destroyed.

The night the Greek troops of Alexander the Great fired the palace of the Achaemenian emperors at Persepolis, a civilization went up in smoke. At the most literal level, of course, it was Persia which suffered. Symbolically, however, this act of gratuitous vandalism can be seen as a defeat for the Greeks themselves, effectively spelling the end to any claim they might have had to a special edifying mission. But while the events of that night in 331BC had indeed brought the reign of the Achaemenians to an abrupt and violent end, the soul of Persia, its culture and spirituality, would survive.

The Persians' holiest book, the *Avesta*, said to have been sumptuously scripted in gold leaf applied to specially prepared oxhides, was long held to have been burned in the fire and its sacred pages lost forever. Some modern scholars, however, believe these scripts were never at Persepolis in the first place, for the holy book of the Zoroastrians would only have existed in oral form at that time.

The myths recorded in the *Avesta* would not be written down by scribes until the sixth century AD, and the oldest versions which survive into our own day date from the thirteenth century AD. Even so, the book provides a remarkable bridge to the remotest reaches of Persia's pagan past. Embedded in the various sections of the *Avesta* – in the great prayers of the *Yasna*, in the "Law against Demons" or *Vendidad*, and in the magnificent hymns of the *Yasht* – are to be found heroic tales of the earliest pagan gods. Many more were recorded by the poet Firdowsi in his epic *Shahnameh*, the "Book of Kings", which he finished in AD1010. But while the heroes of these stories were celebrated as part of the Zoroastrian pantheon, their origins are much older. These texts tell of a time when they ruled as gods in their own right, reflections of a way of life lived at the mercy of the elements and testament to Persia's rich and ancient heritage.

Opposite: A traditional silk Tabriz prayer rug depicting the Saena tree, from the branches of which all life grew.

Below: A page from the *Yasna* section of the *Avesta*, dated 1323.

27

The Valleys of Creation

While the coming of evil shattered the perfect order of the original world, it also provided an essential creative spark: great mountains rose from once flat plains, myriad stars shifted into orbit and invigorating rains began to fall, feeding the bountiful tree of life itself.

The ancient Persians believed their world had originally been a large, flat expanse without mountains, valleys or ravines. It stretched away without feature or flaw to the surrounding sea, windless and unwrinkled by any wave. Nothing changed in this primal perfection and even the sun, stars and moon stood static in the vault of the sky.

This order was hurled into confusion when evil came bursting in upon the world. Like a lightning bolt it tore through the sky and smashed into the Earth. Ripples billowed across the land, forging high mountains and deep valleys. At the point of impact rose Mount Alburz, which for 800 years forged its way upwards to Heaven. From its vertiginous summit arced the bridge by which the souls of the just would one day pass to eternity, while far below wailing sinners would be driven hellwards by mocking demons.

The stars, sun and moon were dislodged from their fixed positions and from that time forth would move without rest across the sky. Their

The south slopes of the Alburz Mountains in Iran, the place where evil first emerged and forged the rugged landscape from the perfect flatness of the first creation.

wanderings, though, would not be aimless, for they were fixed into eternal orbits. Through the cracks the cataclysm had made in the fabric of the heavens, these celestial bodies moved, the sun's circuit delineating day and night and the moon marking the months of the year.

Higher still, beyond Mount Alburz's peak, water formed for the first time. Heavenly winds gathered it up and swept it into a great cosmic ocean, called Vourukasha. From there it fell down to Earth as rain to run through streams to a host of seas. Two great rivers flowed beneath the surface of the Earth, returning rainwater to Vourukasha and completing another new cycle of life.

To the early Persians, therefore, the coming of evil was a stimulus for much in creation. It may have destroyed the blissful changelessness of the

The fish which decorate this 13th-century enamel gilt plate from Persia recall the *kar* which protected the Hom tree, the source of life on Earth. These ten fish were able to defeat the giant lizard that the spirit of evil had sent to destroy creation.

first creation, but it did not unleash anarchy. Rather, it released the dynamic rhythms of the world as we understand them today.

Into this new world came life itself: amid the waters of the Vourukasha grew the Saena tree, or Tree of Many Seeds, whose variegated branches bore the kernels of every different kind of plant. The tree was home to the great Saena bird, and each time it flapped its mighty wings it shook the branches and sent seeds cascading down. In their fertile thousands they fell, to take root in the earth below. One day the spirit of evil sent a giant lizard to attack this source of boundless life, but it was beaten back by the ten fish, or *kar*, which circled the tree's roots to keep it from harm. The essence of the eternal life of the human soul was also kept there, in the mysterious Hom tree, which rose out of Vourukasha's fathomless depths.

Rain from the heavens not merely watered the Earth into teeming life, but helped give it definition too, criss-crossing its surface with rivers and streams which ran into surging seas. Seven separate landmasses, or *kesh-var*, now stood in isolation from each other: the Khvanirath, nearest the Earth's centre, was as large as all the others put together.

Here, on the banks of the River Veh Daiti, grazed the first animal, a mighty bull whose whiteness shone dazzling as the moon. And it was to the moon that this great beast's soul took flight when it was killed in bitter combat with the spirit of evil. From its death came life, its seed dripping down from the heavenly sphere to give rise to every animal species on Earth.

On the other side of the river dwelt the first man, called Gayomartan – but he too would one day fight and lose against the force of evil. His seed, however, would not be destroyed. It rested in the earth for forty years, until it sprang from the ground as a sacred stalk of rhubarb. From its bifurcated form the sacred twins Mashya and Mashyanag were born: the first mortal human beings and the ancestors of us all (see page 63).

29

War at the Heart of Existence

The conflict which raged at the heart of nature was personified in the gods of Persia's pagan pantheon. At its head stood Ahura Mazda, the "Wise Lord" and great creator, ruling over a body of gods who encapsulated the beauty and complexity of the entire universe.

Ahura Mazda lived surrounded by a magnificence of light in the highest place, where no creeping shadows could fall. Far below, beyond a great void, lay a chasm in which Angra Mainyu, the evil one, writhed in darkness. He had chosen a life of wickedness and now, whenever he saw the Wise Lord, the bright beacon of righteousness, far above him, he was driven to attack. In the mighty battles that ensued, however, Ahura Mazda, great creator of the universe and lord of all, would have to turn to a subordinate for help – and would implore Vayu, god of the winds, to ensure his success.

The duality which underpinned all Persia's pre-Muslim theologies is sometimes perplexing. Evil might be as powerful as good, it might even be a constructive force and great gods may need the help of lesser ones to prevail. But oppositions

like these served to express not only all the complex contradictions of existence but also the alternating rhythms by which human life proceeds. And the endless cycles of night and day, of drought and rain, of summer and winter were personified in Persia's many pagan deities.

Of these, Vayu the wind god best represented the oppositions inherent in existence. Though he served as the strong right arm of Ahura Mazda, his territory was actually the void at which good and evil met: war and rivalry were central to his being. But the struggle between good and evil, light and darkness, could never finally be resolved, for this very conflict was the mainspring of existence.

Another of Ahura Mazda's servants was the god of rain, Tishtrya, who appeared in the heavens as the star Sirius. With the refreshing showers he brought from the waters of the Vourukasha ocean, all life on Earth was nurtured and sustained – yet he too had to fight fiercely for every centimetre of Persian ground. The witch Duzhyairya, spirit of bad harvests, was always ready to resist his progress, while in Apaosha, the demon of drought, he had a formidable foe indeed.

A dazzling white horse draped with a golden caparison, Tishtrya would go down to the shores of Vourukasha to gather water each year as the earth grew dry and parched through the summer months – and each year Apaosha, in the guise of a great black horse, would come to challenge him. As he reached his enemy Apaosha would rear up heavenwards, screaming in frenzy as he lashed out

Ahura Mazda's subordinate Vayu graces the face of this coin from the reign of Vasudeva I, c.AD164–200. Vayu was crucial in the fight against Angra Mainyu and his spirits of evil.

The Many Faces of Evil

Evil spirits, or yatu, *could take many different forms, but most belonged to two main types: those which targeted mortals directly, and those which attacked humankind through their livelihood.*

In keeping with the paradoxical nature of Persian dualism, the word *yatu* was used for both evil spirits and the benign sorcerers who fought them. Similarly, the word *div*, or "demon", derived from the old word for "deity". A *div* was therefore a "false god" who interfered with human life. The females, or *pairaka*, were often deadlier than the males: they could fly through the night sky and assume different forms. A rat, a shooting star, even a humble housefly could be a demon in disguise. The virtuous person had to be vigilant at all times.

Bronze winged demon, late Sasanian or early Islamic culture, c.7th-8th century. Evil spirits, however, could take any form.

with his hard hooves. The rain god would be forced into whinnying retreat, and each year called out to Ahura Mazda, complaining that his human worshippers had let him down. Had they honoured him as they ought to have done, with all the sacrifices which had been ordained, he would have had the strength of ten horses, camels and bulls, and ten mountains and rivers, all combined. Not even Apaosha could have prevailed against such a force. Instead, Tishtrya had lost his battle, so the much-needed rains of autumn did not come and each year's drought seemed as if it would never end. Only Ahura Mazda's direct intervention would be strong enough to bring the Earth's suffering to an end.

Eventually the Wise Lord did indeed offer sacrifice to Tishtrya, and the rain god's strength immediately soared. Once again he galloped down to the shores of Vourukasha to raise water, and once more Apaosha came charging out to meet him. This time, however, the horse of light conquered his dark opponent with ease, trampling him beneath his hooves and neighing loudly in triumph. Immediately the cosmic ocean began to boil, sending great banks of vapour billowing upwards; Tishtyra gathered them all together and shepherded them earthwards with strong winds.

Starving peasants rejoiced as they saw the great clouds marshalling on the horizon. As the storm broke they offered heartfelt thanks to Tishtrya and to Ahura Mazda, making all the offerings they could to their sacred gods.

Once again the rains had come to their rescue. Thanks to Ahura Mazda, Tishtrya had once more prevailed. But everyone knew that the victory was far from everlasting. Though defeated for now, Apaosha would surely return: in a year's time the battle would have to be fought anew.

The Goddess and the Warrior

Two great deities typified the contradictory nature of ancient Persian belief. Anahita was at once the gentle goddess of fertility and a vengeful wager of war, both giver and taker of life. And while Verethragna was known to all as the triumphant god of victory, he could be worshipped in at least ten different forms – from youth to bull, raven to ram.

All the life in the universe began and ended with Anahita, for she was the goddess of water, originating spirit of the Vourukasha sea. She was the source of all the streams which coursed down Mount Alburz to the cosmic ocean; she was the fount of all the fertility these waters released on Earth. No more benign or nurturing goddess than Anahita could be imagined – and yet this formidable figure was anything but motherly in her aspect.

Four snorting white horses hauled her chariot as she went tearing across the heavens in a storm of spray: Wind, Rain, Cloud and Sleet were their names and they obscured the sky and cast a chill upon the Earth. Proud and tall amid the swirling mist rode the radiant Anahita herself, an awe-inspiring warrior-woman, as terrifying as she was beautiful. Tall and statuesque she stood, her noble origins evident in her appearance, her haughty authority made clear and commanding through a pair of flashing eyes. A crown of shining gold ringed her royal temples, bejewelled with eight sun-rays and 100 stars: it held her lustrous hair back from her stunning features but did not stop it streaming out behind as she swept onwards across the sky. Squares of gold adorned her ears, a wondrous necklace hung around her neck; her shapely shoulders were clad in a mantle miraculously embroidered with golden thread. With one hand she controlled her team of galloping horses which she urged on to ever-greater speed, in the other she carried the bundle of holy branches which were the sacred symbol of her divine power.

Like so much in early Persian mythology, the idea of such a warlike life-giver seems paradoxical to the modern mind. Yet Anahita's twofold role was logical enough. As goddess of fertility and life

she was worshipped by those who faced death on the battlefield. Hence her invocation by the mythic heroes in the great Avestan prayer, the *Aban Yasht.*

Yet Anahita was revered by spirits of good and evil alike: the demonic forces of the *Avesta* honoured her with sacrifices and implored her for help in their moments of greatest need. The ancient Persians always tended to see their age-old conflict with the northerly kingdom of Turan in terms of the symbolic struggle between good and evil. In the *Aban Yasht,* the king of darkness, the murderous Turanian ruler Afrasiab, is seen making just such sacrifices to Anahita.

The Faces of Victory

Just as ambiguous was the figure of Verethragna, the warrior god of victory. The *Bahram Yasht* lists no fewer than ten distinct physical forms he can assume. In one guise he is a rushing wind; in another a powerful white bull with yellow ears and golden horns. As a white horse with golden caparison he stands for speed and dynamism in war; as a rutting camel he symbolizes sexual energy and masculine power. As a charging boar he is the best-armed and most fearful of gods; as a fifteen-year-old youth, he is physical perfection. Verethragna floats effortlessly aloft as a raven; races across the earth in the form of a running ram; and fights with all the ferocity of the antlered buck. In his tenth guise he is a man with a long sword of glistening gold: a fitting symbol of surpassing virility and irresistible strength.

Verethragna's incarnation as a soaring raven was particularly popular. A bird of ill omen in many other cultures, the raven acquired for the ancient Persians an extraordinary talismanic force. If a man were to hold the bone or feather of that bird, Ahura Mazda once explained, Verethragna's great strength would flow into his limbs: no man would be able to land a blow on him, or turn him to abject flight. Instead, with the god of victory's divine assistance, he would scatter all before him in battle, winning homage from the proudest enemy, prevailing over the mightiest foe. If Persians honoured Verethragna with appropriate sacrifices,

said the great creator, their kingdom would be preserved from every danger. If, on the other hand, they neglected their duties, or if murderous or whorish hands were to defile the god's offerings or altars, then the consequences would be terrible indeed. Evil spirits would rampage throughout the land; plague would flourish and enemies would pour across every border to loot and murder unhindered. Verethragna, it seemed, was to be appeased at all costs.

Mithra's Trusty Guardian

Mithra was the glorious sun god of Persian mythology. Serving as an escort at his side was a fierce boar – a manifestation of Verethragna himself.

The boar flew into battle before the sun god, bringing him victory in every fight. With his sharp fangs and steely tusks he could kill at a single nonchalant blow, while his hooves and jaw of iron made him an irresistible war machine. The merest toss of his heavy head sent mighty warriors flying through the air in all directions; his scything tusks felled the enemy ranks as though they were so many stalks of grain. Those unfortunate enough to fall before him were gored and trampled as he ran forwards into a reeking mire of blood and brains mixed with ground-up bones and tufts of matted hair.

The Gods of Ritual

The world of the gods may have seemed far away, but it could be accessed through the ancient rituals surrounding fire and the sacred drink *haoma*. The divine beings themselves could be conjured from the twisting flames of a votive pyre, while *haoma*'s intoxicating juice could produce visions of divinity that brought to Earth the essential mysteries of life.

Humankind's companion for countless millennia, fire has yet remained something less than a true friend. Although it is a force much used domestically, this mesmerizing element retains a streak of something ungovernably wild. The servant who meekly cooks his master's meals can turn on him, inflicting hideous injuries. Knocked from its perch, the lamp which lights the house at night can start a conflagration in which the whole house is destroyed. The guardian which as a torch can ward off the threat of predators may also rampage indiscriminately through a sleeping village.

These contradictory properties meant that fire, a source of fascination to all peoples in history, exercised a particular hold over the ancient Persians, with their profoundly dualistic view of the world. In its vitality they found an image for the force which animated the universe as a whole: struck out of nothing, a spark could be caught on a piece of kindling and coaxed into something remarkably like life. That fire resonated deeply with the divine was confirmed by the fact that its flames seemed to strain ever upwards towards the sky, as if it sensed that there its true home was at last to be found. A mystical threshold between humanity and the gods, it consumed earthly offerings before sending them heavenwards in the form of smoke. Fire was

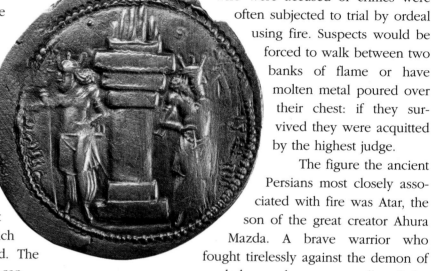

Worshippers at a fire altar, from the reverse side of a coin belonging to the Sasanian king Shapur I, c.AD241–272.

even used to administer justice: those who were accused of crimes were often subjected to trial by ordeal using fire. Suspects would be forced to walk between two banks of flame or have molten metal poured over their chest: if they survived they were acquitted by the highest judge.

The figure the ancient Persians most closely associated with fire was Atar, the son of the great creator Ahura Mazda. A brave warrior who fought tirelessly against the demon of darkness, he was an ally of the glorious Mithra, mighty god of the sun. Atar rode behind Mithra's fiery chariot, while Verethragna, in his guise as a boar, galloped on ahead (see box, page 33). It was in the heroic defence of Mithra's divine glory that Atar's most celebrated exploit was performed, when his lord came under attack from the diabolical monster, Azhi Dahaka. The epic battle that followed is described in the *Avesta*'s *Zamyad Yasht*.

With three mouths spouting every conceivable blasphemy set in three heads thinking every evil thought, Azhi was the most powerful embodiment of evil and destruction imaginable: if any *div* could extinguish Mithra's divine glory it would be he. His six eyes saw all that existed in creation; his 1,000 senses knew everything as it occurred. His terrible appearance filled all with dread, and the fire god was no exception. Atar could not help flinching as he saw Azhi launch himself at Mithra, attempting to wrest the divine flame from his noble hand. The demon spoke to him disdainfully, warning him he would extinguish his light for ever if he attempted to intervene on his lord's behalf. But Atar boldly advanced on the attacker, warning him that he would blaze up through his loins and flare out through his threefold throat if he did not leave his master Mithra alone. Now it was Azhi Dahaka's turn to cringe in terror: he hung his heads and slunk sheepishly from the field. The divine glory was safe, thanks to the courage of the warrior Atar.

In another celebrated exploit, Atar came to the rescue of the world when a *div* was delaying the onset of the annual rains. Taking on the form of a bolt of lightning, he flashed towards the earth to strike the demon down: the obstruction removed, the moisture-laden clouds were able to advance unhindered. What to us seems a strange alliance of fire and water in this myth reminds us once again that the oppositions underpinning the ancient Persian universe were not our own. Darkness and death were the eternal enemy of humankind, and fire was among the strongest symbols of light and life. Its most sacred role was as the banisher of dark spirits.

Fires of Eternal Light

In Sasanian times three "eternal" fires were kept permanently alight – one for each estate of society: warriors, priests and workers. These fires reflected the glory of the social classes. Foreigners and non-Zoroastrians, however, would claim that the Persians worshipped fire itself. This suggestion was angrily rejected, despite the continuing centrality of fire in Zoroastrian ritual.

Haoma, the Divine Hallucinogen

Although its juice oozed yellow as the rays of the sun, as liquid as the life-giving rain, the drink which was extracted from the haoma plant had qualities more divine by far than these.

Poets and priests alike found ecstatic inspiration in the extravagant visions it brought and warriors were prompted to deeds of astonishing bravery in battle. With such properties it was a god among plants and it naturally acquired its own associated deity: the god Haoma, lord of harvests.

Those who were offered a hint of Heaven under the influence of the divine drink called upon Haoma himself for happiness and health on Earth. They also asked for longevity to appreciate these precious gifts, and for sons and daughters so that countless generations could enjoy them too.

Nobody knows which drug *haoma* was in reality, though the Zoroastrians seem to have used a type of ephedrine for a similar purpose. When *haoma* was drunk, it induced a trance-like state in which the boundaries of everyday reality melted before the drinker's eyes to be supplanted with myriad visions of divinity. The substance was thus a key part of religious ritual.

Sasanian or early Islamic dark green glass stem cup, 5th–7th century AD.

The First Earthly Kings

If all the positive forces of the universe were wielded by the gods, it took mortal kings to forge the foundations of human civilization. But with the steady accumulation of knowledge in arts as varied as cooking, weaving and the taming of animals came the need to defend the fledgling culture from the destructive attentions of evil spirits.

According to Firdowsi's *Shahnameh*, Kiyumars was the first mortal king. He was all but godly in his powers and looked down upon the world from his throne at the top of a high mountain. He introduced many things to the world: his leopardskin robes were the first clothes, the food his people collected the first human nourishment.

His reign lasted thirty years, during which time all nature and humanity came to pay homage to him. His virtues blazed forth across the world like a generous sun; his purity shone out like the moon over a swaying cypress. The very notion of reverence began with Kiyumars, for his was the idea that men and women should strive for earthly perfection following heavenly laws. He it was who introduced humankind to religion.

The world prospered in his care, and peace reigned for many a long year, but though temporarily checked by his glorious virtues, the forces of evil could not be kept at bay for ever. The battle to save his kingdom would be bloody and protracted, but Kiyumars and his descendants would rise to this most demanding challenge.

The first assault on his happy realm came from the Black Demon, son of the great evil spirit Ahriman (the equivalent of the *Avesta*'s Angra Mainyu). The Black Demon murdered Kiyumars' son Siyamak, and nearly broke the king's heart. But Kiyumars composed himself and summoned his grieving grandson, Hushang. He told the brave young man that the death had to be avenged, but warned him that he himself would be killed in the coming conflict and that upon Hushang would fall the responsibilities of king.

All this did indeed come to pass. In the battle that ensued, Hushang struck down his father's killer, cut off the *div*'s head and trampled it disdainfully into the mud. With his own life's work brought to fruition by his grandson's great deed, Kiyumars died there and then, and Hushang respectfully took his crown. As he ascended the

The *Shahnameh* says that Kiyumars, shown in this 19th-century watercolour, was the first mortal king. He was famed for introducing many useful things to the world, including clothing.

throne the young man announced a new dispensation for humankind. Striving by superior craft and cunning, he said, humanity was destined to tame the wild Earth.

Hushang wasted no time inaugurating this new order. First he found a miraculous touchstone by which iron ore might be extracted from the rock in which it lay. Mastering all the arts of metalworking, he made tools, weapons and containers. With axes and saws to build their houses and implements to open up the earth, Hushang's people were in a position to bring the world's first civilization into being. By long networks of channels and ditches they drew water from the rivers to irrigate fields they had learned to sow with seeds. The first hoes made cultivation easy; sharp sickles helped gather in the harvest. Animals were tamed and set to work, hauling and carrying on behalf of humanity, or simply grazing in the fields until they were needed for meat, hide and wool. Spinning and weaving were now possible, and proper clothing could be made. Where once men and women had lived in ignorance and fear like animals, they now shaped their world with confidence and pride.

King Hushang also discovered the secret of making fire and harnessing its power. One day, when the king was out hunting in the mountains with his attendant lords, he saw a great monster rushing down the rocky slope towards them. It was black and fierce, with eyes like pools of blood and a mouth from which dense smoke poured. His courtiers shrank back in fear but Hushang held his ground. He calmly picked up a stone from the ground and hurled it at the strange beast. Although it seemed untouched, the black fiend swerved away – but not before the king had seen a vital truth. Where his missile struck the monster's stony

hide a spark had flashed – the birth of all future fire. Hushang fell to his knees to thank his creator for the secret he had shown him: from that time forth humanity would have fire at its command. It would be their link with divinity.

Of Hushang's successor, Tahmuras, comparatively little is known, except that he fought valiantly to free humanity from the manacles of evil and ignorance. He drove out demons and black magic, ending idolatry and establishing an age of wisdom and truth. Beyond that, he remains an insubstantial figure. Tahmuras's most celebrated act, however, was his victory over the arch-demon Ahriman. Turning the vanquished king of evil into a horse, he forced his tossing head into a bridle, saddled him up and then rode him round the Earth for thirty years. Only when the desperate Ahriman had sworn to vouchsafe the secret arts of literacy did Tahmuras finally free the demon from his servitude.

Gold and silver statuette of a horse, Persian, c.14th–15th century. Tahmuras rode the demon Ahriman as a steed for 30 years until the secret arts of literacy were divulged.

Years of Peace and Plenty

In some accounts the greatest of the Persian kings was Yima, whose 1,000-year reign was a time of unsurpassed peace and prosperity. With the blessing of the great god Ahura Mazda, this triumphant ruler also thwarted the wicked designs of Angra Mainyu.

According to Firdowsi, Tahmuras was succeeded by his son Jamshid. The *Avesta*, however, claims that Persia's greatest king was Yima, and this account also suggests that the manifold advances of human civilization were the achievements not of Hushang or Jamshid, but of Yima alone.

The *Avesta* describes Yima's 1,000-year reign as a golden age of ease and abundance. Entrusted with the rule of the whole world by Ahura Mazda, Yima vowed to protect his kingdom from all harm. While he was king, he told his divine master, no chill wind would ever blow, nor would any scorching scirocco sear the earth. Disease and death would both be strangers to a world in which everything was good, and no *div* would ever dare to show his face.

Ahura Mazda was pleased and gave his king a golden ring and dagger to seal his sovereignty. Yima did not disappoint him. Under his rule the world prospered as never before. Men and women, birds and animals all thrived, and the population rose rapidly year after year.

By the time 300 winters had passed, however, the Earth could no longer hold all its creatures and the idyll seemed poised to turn into a nightmare.

Ahura Mazda sought to warn his king of the danger, but he found him quite unfazed: Yima merely took his ring and dagger and pressed them into the ground. Then he commanded the Earth to open and outstretch itself, that there might be room for its population. The ground beneath him creaked and shuddered in response and was riven from side to side by a mighty chasm. The horizons seemed to retreat on every front as the world extended itself by a third. Now it seemed there would be ample space for any number of human and animal inhabitants.

Twice more the world was filled to bursting and each time Yima pushed his gold ring into the ground and stuck his dagger into the soil, commanding the world to stretch to accommodate its people. And each time the mighty Earth obeyed his command and extended its wide horizons.

Three Deadly Winters

Such incomparable felicity could not endure unchallenged. The lord of evil looked on Yima's world with bitterness in his heart. He was sickened by the sight of such bounty and he determined to spread suffering throughout the land with three terrible winters in which each and every beast would wither up and freeze.

The great creator, Ahura Mazda, however, knew of these evil designs and instructed Yima to build a great *vara*, or compound, in which the essential components of life might ride out the deathly storm in warmth and security. In this enclosure, some two kilometres square, Yima was to bring together the seeds of every different kind of plant and animal. Cattle, horses, sheep and goats and every type of farmyard fowl – all domestic animals and birds were to be represented, for there would be space for everything to thrive and multiply beyond winter's icy reach. The creator then bade Yima divert streams, raise banks and carve out valleys, so that every type of landscape might be found in the *vara*. Thus would he reproduce the habitats favoured by all the species of wild animal and bird on Earth.

There was to be a miniature city too, at the very centre of the *vara*: nine criss-crossing streets in which a human populace might reproduce and grow. The seeds of men and women were to be carefully selected, so that no physical deformity or moral weakness might be admitted, for they were the brands of Angra Mainyu on the bodies and minds of humanity.

Yima did as he was instructed, completing his preparations just as the chill wind of the first great winter began to blow. Sealing the entrance with his sacred ring of gold, he sat back safe within his *vara*'s secure confines to watch and wait while blizzards blasted the world beyond. Outside, the Earth sickened and died, but here a little community of seeds was growing amid warmth and sunshine, a new world of humans, plants and animals slowly taking shape.

Three years later the storms abated and an expectant hush descended upon the Earth; Yima pushed open the gate of his compound to look out upon an eerily empty and sterile scene. The jostling energy crammed in behind

A Persian knife, c.19th century. When Yima struck the soil with his dagger, the Earth stretched and made more land for his crowded civilization.

39

Nature's bounty is celebrated in this 17th-century Persian painting. Yima's *vara*, like Noah's ark, ensured that the plants and animals of the creation survived potential disaster.

the shady depths of its virgin forests. Birds dived and soared, enjoying the vast empty space of its open skies. Men and women meanwhile went out to colonize the Earth, building cities and societies from first principles. And all rejoiced that the whole world had been saved by Yima's action in building his great *vara*.

Jamshid's Golden Age

In the *Shahnameh*'s version, the Earth first flourished during the reign of Jamshid. The key to the success of his governership, however, was his ability to fashion iron into instruments of war. He devoted the first fifty years of his reign to arming the people and protecting his realm from attack. Helmets, chain-mail and other armour as well as arrows and swords were made in their thousands and stored up in case they should be needed.

For the next half-century of his rule he turned his attention to clothing of more pacific kinds, developing the different skills associated with the cultivation and weaving of textiles. That task completed, he set about moulding humanity itself into a coherent whole. His first undertaking was to appoint the various estates of society. He established the priesthood to oversee the relationship of men and women to the gods; he made a class of warriors to protect society from its enemies. A caste of small farmers was also created. They were poor and fiercely independent, but their tireless labours created prosperity for all. The fourth class Jamshid established was the craftsmen, trained to work to the highest standards, fashioning items both for beauty and use.

him could not be contained for long, however: life came surging forth to revitalize the waiting world. In places carpeted with grass and flowers, elsewhere thick with shrubs and trees, the landscape soon resembled a fresher version of its former self. Grazing flocks and herds tasted the pristine pasture of its undulating plains; wild animals explored

40

The First New Year

When Jamshid was still more concerned with the creator's glory than with his own, he willed a marvellous new throne into being with the force of his divinely inspired command, ushering in a new and glorious era.

Jamshid ordered a horde of demon slaves to raise his new throne high into the air. Then he sat upon it and shone down on the Earth with all the refulgent brilliance of a second sun.

That day, the first on which the divine glory had truly been seen on Earth, was regarded as the start of a new epoch for the world. Ever after on that same day – the day of the spring solstice, 21 March in the modern Western calendar – people celebrated the beginning of the Persian New Year. Maintained in Zoroastrian times, and on through the Islamic era, the festival of Now Ruz remains the most important in Iran and is honoured throughout much of Central Asia.

Dividing up the responsibilities and privileges of the world justly among all the Earth's inhabitants, he also gave animals, birds and spirits their allotted place. Even the evil *div* were given a task: they had to make bricks and construct great buildings from stone. He found precious metals and minerals in the earth, and beautiful balms and fragrances in nature. He invented the ship, and sailed to every corner of his kingdom: no place in the whole wide world could now remain uncharted. Jamshid bestowed every skill of civilization on his fortunate subjects – and with demons for slaves there was no need for them to consider the indignities of labour.

Yet both Yima and Jamshid brought their respective golden ages to an end by their own sinful pride, for their greatness lifted them above every human vice save that of vanity. Yima, in the Avestan tradition, is said to have started claiming divine qualities for himself, forgetting that he was Ahura Mazda's instrument, not his equal.

He began to lie, and increasingly to set falsehood before truth. His own reputation, rather than the divine glory, became his chief preoccupation. The celestial energy with which Ahura Mazda had filled him when the creator set him up on his throne now left him: it could be seen taking flight from his body, soaring heavenwards in the form of a great bird. His mortality confirmed, Yima was soon killed by the evil dragon Azhi Dahaka, who took his unfortunate kingdom – and his two fair daughters – for himself.

Jamshid's disgrace was comparable. He too began arrogating the glory of the gods to himself. His priests and nobles listened appalled as, carried away by pride and lust for power, he boldly asserted his own godly power. None dared object to what he said, but he was reduced in the eyes of all by his vainglory – and from that time forth the world he had built began to fall apart. The loyalty of his people ebbed away; respect for the king and the laws he stood for went into steep decline. Anarchy gripped his realm as his own authority waned; the kingdom he had built so painstakingly dissolved into discord.

With his power and glory gone Jamshid, like Yima, was easy prey to the vengeful forces of evil. According to Firdowsi, Jamshid was sawn in two by the serpent-shouldered King Zahak who then usurped his kingdom. Thus the two kings came to similar ends. On the fates of Jamshid and Yima, then, the accounts of the *Shahnameh* and the earlier *Avesta* for once agree.

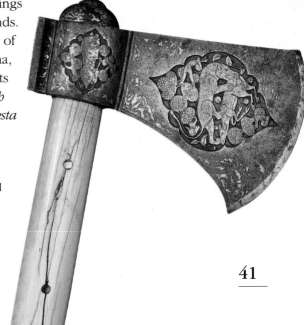

A fine Persian engraved and damascened axehead, c.18th century. Jamshid's golden age was maintained by his prowess at making tools of war.

A Perfect Prince Beguiled

Like King Jamshid before him, Zahak was born a noble hero and died a pitiful sinner. His decline, however, was far more precipitous and sinister. Led astray by vanity, Zahak proved easy prey to vengeful spirits who punished him with the strangest of fates.

In the desert kingdom of Arabia, peopled by spear-brandishing warriors who rode swift horses, lived the pious King Merdas with his beloved son Zahak. As noble and godfearing as his father, this fine youth surpassed him in every other respect. Stunningly handsome and breathtakingly accomplished, he was courageous and skilled in combat. His horsemanship was quite unrivalled, for he spent two-thirds of his life in the saddle, riding about his father's realm on errands of generosity. No vice or failing seemed to mar the impression of perfection he made wherever he went.

Zahak watches Jamshid's execution, from an 18th-century illustrated version of the _Shahnameh_. Zahak himself was led to an untimely and humiliating end as a result of his own vanity.

Like those other paragons, Yima and Jamshid, however, he was open to one temptation – that of vanity. The devil saw this and determined to exploit it in his bid to rid the world of its bountiful creations. Assuming human form, he posed as a visitor to the court and set about winning Zahak over with fulsome flattery and praise. The innocent boy was deceived with ease.

Once the devil had his unbounded confidence, he explained his wicked plan. The king his father was old and useless, the devil said: should not Zahak himself by now be occupying his throne? And if Merdas would not pass on through natural causes, should he not be assisted by other, more drastic means? But even as he rejected the foul scheme in outrage and indignation, Zahak found himself faltering in his resolve. He was soon set on usurping his father's throne.

So it was that the next evening found him in a quiet arbour of the palace garden where his father was accustomed to going at nightfall for private prayer. Just where the path was darkest, winding through dense shrubbery, the devil had dug a deep pit into which the pious old king fell and died. Seizing his late father's crown, Zahak ascended the murdered man's throne. He had his wish – he was ruler in his father's place.

A Curse upon his Shoulders

Zahak did his best to discharge his duty as a worthy monarch. But the devil had plans of his own. One morning he presented himself at court again, this time in the form of a personable and plausible young man. He was, he told the king, a cook of the utmost renown – but no honour could be higher than that of serving Zahak. Flattered by these warm words, the young ruler agreed to take him on – and it was not long before he was rejoicing at his decision. His new cook had a truly gifted cunning with food, serving up old familiar dishes with new zest and panache. Entranced by such pleasures, the king offered his new cook whatever his heart desired. Only this, the young man said, that you should allow me to embrace you once as

Two snakes entwined in battle, from a detail of a manuscript attributed to the artist Haribans, c.1603.

an equal, even though we both know I am not of appropriate rank. Bewitched by luxury, King Zahak had no thought for social proprieties: he agreed to the cook's odd request without hesitation. So, stepping up to his royal master, the cook took him in his arms, embraced him, and then vanished into the ground.

Zahak scarcely had time to register his astonishment before something still more amazing happened: from each shoulder where the cook had kissed him a hissing black serpent appeared. He lashed out with his hands and rolled on the floor in vain attempts to dislodge them; he had them cut off but new ones simply sprang up in their place. Physicians flocked from far and wide, but none was able to rid him of his writhing attendants. Finally, though, a venerable old doctor appeared at the court. There was no hope of removing the serpents, said the sage, but their insatiable hunger might at least be pacified if they were fed on an exclusive diet of human brains. The physician, of course, was the demon, in yet another disguise. Zahak, driven to distraction by the serpents on his shoulders, ordered the treatment to commence.

Soon afterwards, the knights of Persia begged Zahak to come and relieve them of their once-revered king, Jamshid. They would have ample opportunity to rue their eagerness afterwards. Zahak vanquished Jamshid with ease, then had the fallen hero sawn in half. But Zahak's reign was a 1,000-year curse, a chaotic age of murder, oppression, lies and misery unbounded. And, of course, every single day for a millennium, young men were sacrificed to the snakes which coiled and hissed on King Zahak's cursed shoulders.

43

The Slayer of Demons

Thraetaona was revered as the great dragon-slayer of the *Avesta*, but he also became known as an accomplished physician, for when he released the world from tyranny by killing Azhi Dahaka, he also cured himself of the many ailments that had dogged his life.

Azhi Dahaka was created by Angra Mainyu to wage war on righteousness and truth. He was a hideous beast to behold and still more terrible to engage in battle. His three heads bobbed and wove confusingly on three long and scaly necks and his three jaws were lined with terrifying fangs. He had been beaten once, by brave Atar, but the defeat had left the monster nursing a still more implacable rage and he was bent on revenge.

As Azhi stormed ever more destructively back and forth across the universe, the creator resolved that his rampage should be ended once and for all. Calling Thraetaona to his presence, he told him what it was that he required. Thraetaona at once invoked the assistance of the divine Anahita, sacrificing 100 stallions, 1,000 oxen and 10,000 lambs to her honour.

The water goddess listened to his requests and resolved to help him. When Azhi Dahaka mounted his first furious attack, Thraetaona, filled with divine energy, stood firm – he even met the dragon's onslaught with a stinging blow of his own. As the fiend swooped again and again, the hero succeeded in landing still more blows on his attacker's body. The demon had met its match.

Thraetaona's skill, however, was ill-rewarded, for from every wound he made in the dragon's scaly skin a stream of loathsome creatures came flowing forth: snakes, toads, lizards, frogs and scorpions, and every manner of repulsive pest. But the hero acted quickly: rather than wound Azhi Dahaka further he decided to disable his hideous enemy and take him, bound and helpless, to Mount Demavand. There he imprisoned him deep inside the peak's rocky mass. Safe at last, Azhi Dahaka's own prisoners now emerged: the two beautiful daughters of Yima, Savanghavak and Erenavak, who gave themselves to Thraetaona as wives in gratitude.

Thraetaona's triumph over Azhi Dahaka was a victory over his various ailments too: from that time onwards he was revered not only as a warrior-hero but as a divine physician.

This story is echoed in the *Shahnameh* with Azhi Dahaka anthropomorphized as Zahak and Thraetaona recreated as Faridun. Firdowsi's account, however, differs greatly in the details.

Mount Demavand, where Thraetaona successfully imprisoned the hideous demon-snake Azhi Dahaka.

The Division of the Kingdom

As so often in the stories of the Shahnameh, Faridun's 500-year reign was to end in acrimony and discord. The cause of the chaos was not corruption, however, but his misguided attempts to distribute his inheritance fairly between his sons.

Two warriors on horseback clash, school of Tabriz, c.1480. Much of Persian myth was defined by conflict and bitter rivalry between kings.

While the two elder boys, Salm and Tur, were given western Persia and Central Asia respectively, the youngest, his father's favourite, was given Iran. Their resentment boiling over, Salm and Tur rounded on their brother and killed him, plunging the world into an age of evil and bitter war. Persia and the northern kingdom of Tur remained locked in conflict for centuries, with many great heroes fighting countless battles.

Thus fratricide forms the central tragedy of Firdowsi's epic history, the consequences of which resounded through many generations.

One night, Zahak dreamed that a child, called Faridun, had been born in his land and that this boy would one day murder him. As soon as he awoke he sent out assassins with instructions to find and kill the child. They soon came close, capturing and killing Faridun's father, but his mother fled with his brothers to the Alburz Mountains where she brought up her sons in hiding. Zahak's agents continued their search, but in vain.

One day, the king was confronted in his own court by an old man, Kaveh, who came to voice a grievance. Seventeen sons of his had been slaughtered to have their brains fed to the serpents on Zahak's shoulders – and now it seemed it was to be the turn of his beloved youngest son. It was too

much, he told the astonished king: he had a right to demand that his last surviving child should be spared. Astonished at the old man's forthrightness in a court where flattery was the common currency, the king's attendants were too stunned to stop Kaveh speaking. They were still more amazed when their king meekly obliged, ordering that the boy be brought forth and restored to his father. He attached no conditions to his release, he said, but he did entreat one favour. Handing the old man his proclamation, he requested that he add his signature. But he was reckoning without the straightforward honesty of this humble, simple man: rising up in anger, Kaveh tore the proclamation into pieces. Then, pushing his son before him, he

Keresaspa – Saviour of Creation

Unmistakable in his curly sidelocks, the youthful Keresaspa was in some ways the most fully human of the Avestan heroes, appealing in his dashing manner and his easy-going ways. Yet these very qualities would one day prove his undoing.

Though he killed many terrible monsters and preserved the world from countless evil attacks, Keresaspa was not as observant of the ritual pieties as he ought to have been. So when he approached the glorious portals of the heavenly sanctuary after his death, the great creator refused him entry. Only after interventions from the other gods and heroes, who pleaded eloquently and passionately with their lord, did Ahura Mazda finally rule that he might be admitted after all.

And yet this spiritual scape-grace was marked down by destiny to save the world, returning from death in the Earth's hour of greatest need. At the end of time, the myth insists, Azhi Dahaka will break free from the prison in which Thraetaona placed him, returning to harrow humanity and destroy creation.

His work of many ages on the point of destruction, Ahura Mazda will have no alternative then but to recall from the dead the greatest warrior of all time. Keresaspa will sweep swiftly down from Heaven and smite the demon dragon with his mighty club. Only then will the terrible curse of evil be ended, once and for all.

strode out into the street, leaving a court dumbfounded both by the old man's courage and by their king's unusual passivity.

When they asked their lord why he had not had this insolent commoner struck down on the spot, Zahak confessed that Kaveh's very presence had unnerved him. As the smith spoke a mountain of iron had seemed to spring up before the king's eyes. When he had struck his head with his hand in anger, this mountain had seemed to shatter. What this strange vision portended, Zahak said, he could not possibly imagine: yet he was sure that it was no trivial thing.

So indeed it was to prove for, having marched straight to the city square, Kaveh began calling the Persian people to arms. Lashing his leather blacksmith's apron to the end of a spear, he raised high this banner of popular power and set off through the city ahead of a growing crowd. Through the countryside they marched, their columns ever-burgeoning as people flocked to join them from near and far, brandishing tools and improvised weapons as they went. Into the Alburz Mountains Kaveh led the way until they reached the secluded castle where Faridun was hiding, now grown into a bold and handsome young man. Receiving this ragged army with the utmost courtesy, the prince accepted Kaveh's leather banner with real pride. He had it decorated with dazzling jewels and bedecked with brightly coloured ribbons.

Calling his brothers to him, he asked that they have a mace fashioned for him: a massive weapon in the form of a bull's head. Thus armed, he set off at the head of Kaveh's army to return to the city which had so briefly been his home.

When the ramparts came in sight he urged his charger forwards. Fire burst spontaneously from his terrifying figure and as he waved his mace in anger it seemed as if all creation trembled. The sentries on the city walls took flight and Faridun burst into the streets within, putting all Zahak's knights and courtiers to the sword. Then he fell upon the king's steward, Kondrun, who explained that Zahak was not to be found. He then offered the hero the finest produce from the royal cellars.

At dawn, as Faridun slept off his celebratory meal, Kondrun rode off to where his lord was staying and told him of the prince who had come to usurp his throne. The serpent king flew into a fury, blaming his steward for the misfortune. Kondrun would listen to these ignorant rantings no longer and, deciding that his days as Zahak's servant were done, he fled into the countryside alone.

Without his wise assistant, Zahak's position grew ever weaker: he led his army aimlessly back to the city without strategy or plan. There he found all the people risen up against him and his force depleted by desertions. Undaunted, Zahak strode into the palace to confront his usurper. Whirling his bull's-head club, Faridun landed a mighty blow on the serpent-king's head, shattering his helmet to smithereens. As he moved in to deliver the final blow, an angel appeared and stopped him: the tyrant should not be killed yet, he said, but taken to a place in the mountains.

In accordance with the angel's wishes, Faridun tied Zahak securely before mounting the throne and declaring the hostilities over. Persia's common people had done heroic work, he said, but now it was time for them to return to their allocated trades, for they would now be able to prosper. All received his proclamation with a heartfelt cheer. Zahak was then led in bonds to Mount Demavand and left on some forsaken slope to die in chains. Faridun was now king, and order and contentment returned once more to the world.

A traditional Persian mace. Whirling such a club, Faridun smote Zahak, shattering his helmet into pieces.

THE BOUNTY OF PARADISE

Amid the arid Iranian deserts of old few things were as treasured as gardens which promised water and shade, and plants that offered medicinal balm. These fruits of nature have been central to Persia since the dawn of time: myths claimed that the first humans were nurtured by rhubarb and sustained by *haoma* (see page 35), while Zoroaster taught that the blessed would find life beyond death in a shady, perfumed garden.

The image of the walled garden dates back to the early days of cultivation. Its memory haunts the Koran whose stories linger in groves of cypress and plane trees, where the taste of orange and smell of rose and jasmine hang all around. The Persians were the first to realize the idyllic potential of such places, and their gardens, secluded from the desert beyond their bounds, have given the Western world a vision of Eden itself: for from the Old Persian *paridaida* – meaning "encircled garden or park" – our word "paradise" derives.

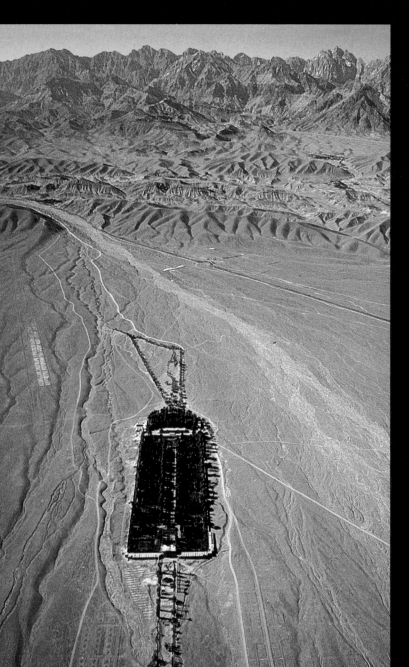

Above: The Narinjistan (Orangerie), built in the 1880s at Shiraz, is a typical Persian garden. Water and coloured flowers dominate, while paths lined with orange trees emphasize the garden's role in pleasuring all senses: sight, smell, taste and even touch.

Left: The Bagh-e Shahzadeh, near Mahan, shows how Persian gardens were able to make such an extraordinary impression on visitors. It is watered by *qanat*, underground channels which have brought rainwater down from the distant mountains since the 6th century BC. Legend credits Hushang, Kiyumars' grandson, with creating irrigation.

Left: An illustration from a 15th-century *Shahnameh* shows people enjoying the shade of a garden. Such is the detail of this kind of artwork that individual plants and flowers are clearly visible, including flowering almond trees, hollyhocks, irises and violets. The desert is just visible beyond the boundary, suggesting the harsh, inhospitable world outside.

Below: The work of such men as Ibn Sina (see box, page 21) had a profound impact on the understanding of medicine around the world. His investigations were based on the curative properties of herbs, and he would have used tools similar to this 13th-century silver and copper mortar and pestle from Khorasan, northeastern Persia. Herbal medicine has an important place in mythology as well as history, for the *Avesta* tells how Ameretat, protector of plants, first brought healing herbs to the world (see page 62).

THE FLAMES OF WISDOM

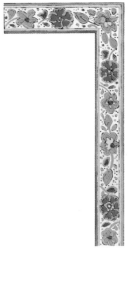

The life of the Persian prophet Zarathustra, known in the West by the Greek form Zoroaster, is lost to history. What little is known comes from seventeen *Gatha*, or hymns, found in the *Avesta*, the sacred book of Zoroastrianism, the religion based on his teachings. Tradition holds that Zoroaster came from Central Asia or even further north and similarities between the *Gatha* and the ancient Hindu text the *Rig Veda* have led some scholars to date him to around 1500–1200BC. Others believe he lived in the seventh to sixth centuries BC.

According to Zoroastrians, the prophet married and fathered several children but at the age of thirty had a series of visions that inspired him to found a new religious faith. From the *Avesta* it appears that Zoroaster could not establish the new religion in his own land and set out in search of a princely patron. He found such a figure in Vishtaspa (see page 55) whose domain was probably Khorasmia, a region east of the Aral Sea now covered by parts of Uzbekistan, Turkmenistan and Afghanistan.

Zoroaster was steeped in the religious beliefs of the pagan Iranian tribes and he built his new faith upon these foundations. He declared that the traditional opposition between *asha* ("truth") and *druj* ("the lie") was central to all religious activities and all mythology. In the pagan religion the god Mazda was, with Mithra and Apam Napat, one of three *ahura* ("lords") acting as guardians of *asha*. But in Zoroaster's vision Mazda was transformed into the one great creator God, source of all good things and sole master of *asha*.

Under the Sasanians, from the third to the seventh centuries AD, Zoroastrianism was the official religion of the Persian empire. Although it was eclipsed in the wake of the seventh-century Islamic invasion of Persia, it survived and a significant number of followers live in Iran today. Altogether, there are around 200,000 Zoroastrians still worshipping worldwide.

Zoroastrianism also left a remarkable legacy through its influence on other religions. Scholars believe that when Jewish tribes were exiled in Babylon in the sixth century BC they were strongly influenced by Zoroastrianism, and its doctrines fed into Judaism and thence into Christianity. The idea of a Devil opposed to all God's works, of an immortal soul and of a general Day of Judgement following a bodily resurrection – instantly familiar to readers schooled in the Christian tradition – all appear to have parallels in the teachings of Zoroaster.

Opposite: Angels, such as this one painted in Bukhara, *c.*1555, sent rains to carry Zoroaster's body to Earth and instructed him in the ways of good and evil when he got there.

Below: The eternal flame at Atashkad, a fire temple in the ancient town of Yazd, in central Iran. Here, fire captures the essence of divinity.

51

The Birth of Zoroaster

As Zoroastrianism became established, mythical traditions grew up around the life of its
founder, emphasizing the prophet's great holiness. It was held that he had been chosen
by the Wise Lord Ahura Mazda himself to spread wisdom throughout creation.

When the time was ripe for Zoroaster to be born, three aspects of the holy prophet – his heavenly glory, his guardian spirit and his physical body – descended to Earth and planted themselves in a young and pure-hearted Iranian woman named Dughdov. She was just fifteen, the perfect age according to Persian tradition, when she gave birth to the great prophet.

The Wise Lord's heavenly glory, bright as the sun, had already taken its place on the hearthstone of Zoroaster's forbears – and from the fire tended by Dughdov's father it had leaped into his wife's body when she was pregnant with Dughdov. From the day of her birth, the child shone with the light that cannot be doused, bearing witness to her purity and to the glory of Heaven. But people were frightened when they saw her glowing in the dark, and demons persuaded many people that the light showed she was a witch. When Dughdov's father, believing the lie, sent her away from home she found refuge under the roof of the Spitama family. Then the work of the evil force was turned to good, for the exiled Dughdov fell in love with the son of the house, Pourushasp, who was the divinely ordained earthly father of Zoroaster.

The guardian spirit of Zoroaster was carried to Earth by Neryosang, the divine messenger, and Yima, the mythical first king of men; they placed it in a *haoma* plant at the top of a tall tree. The very day after his wedding to Dughdov, Pourushasp was walking by this tree and found the mysterious *haoma*, which he took back to his new wife. The plant released an intoxicating milky juice when crushed. This divine sap played an important role in the religious rituals of the pagan Indo-Iranians – it was offered to the gods and also drunk by priests (see box page 35).

Zoroaster's physical body came to Earth in the form of lightly falling rains sent by Haurvatat and Ameretat, two Holy Immortals or angels (see pages 57–58). Divinely inspired, Pourushasp went to the grasses fed by these heavenly waters with a herd of cows too young to have given birth to calves. Miraculously, these animals produced milk although they had no offspring to feed. When Dughdov drank the milk mixed with the juice of the *haoma* plant, Zoroaster's body immediately took wonderful form in her womb.

The young bride was filled with happiness as the holy child grew within her. On the auspicious day of his birth, a brilliant light shone in Dughdov's house and the brightness of joy flooded through the animals, plants, waters and rocks of Ahura Mazda's good creation – but the demon army of the evil one was engulfed by fear, which welled up like a sea of shadows. The infant Zoroaster laughed. As soon as he was born he was aware of his joyous mission on Earth and spoke directly to Ahura Mazda.

The demons were not slow to launch an attack on Zoroaster, whose perfect goodness they could not endure. They clouded Pourushasp's mind, and the poor man came to believe that his son's radiance was a sign of wickedness. One day the father stole away with the baby and, finding a gloomy place, built a fire on which to burn Zoroaster to death. He stoked the pyre as best he could, but the flames would not harm the child.

Another time Pourushasp left Zoroaster's tiny body on the sunbaked ground and drove a herd of cattle towards him, but the ox at the head of the charge was dazzled by a celestial light shining from the baby's eyes and thundered to a stop. It stood guard over him while the other animals

Visions of the Great Protector

According to tradition, Zoroaster's birth and the wonderful deeds he would perform in Ahura Mazda's name were revealed to a chosen few long before the great prophet was born on Earth.

In the first days, when Angra Mainyu attacked the good and bounteous creation, he slaughtered the first man and bull. The bull's soul flew to the very peak of Heaven where Ahura Mazda sat on a great throne that shone and sparkled with brilliant light. The bull complained to the Wise Lord that it was without a protector and was granted a vision: the celestial soul, or *fravashi*, of the great Zoroaster would one day protect cattle and all of creation, instituting a new era at the end of which evil would be entirely destroyed and the universe be restored to the perfectly good form intended by Ahura Mazda. Gladdened, the bull descended to Earth once more. Later, it revealed the secret of Zoroaster's coming to a mythical Iranian prince named Us.

Yima, who in ancient Indo-Iranian myths was both the first king and ruler of the underworld, was also granted a vision of Zoroaster and the array of deeds he would achieve on Earth.

Another tradition held that the divine light of Ahura Mazda was to be found on Earth long before Zoroaster was born, and that it was handed down from a series of holy men to the prophet. It shone most brightly in the breast of the brave and righteous Zoroaster.

rushed past. Then Pourushasp tried to murder his son with a stampede of horses, but again one of the animals, a fine stallion, protected Zoroaster. Next Pourushasp abandoned the child in wild land close to a wolf's den, but when the she-wolf returned she gently tended the infant.

Evil could not rest in its efforts to do away with good in the form of Zoroaster but every attempt to kill the child failed. He grew up to be a wise, clear-thinking young man who always demonstrated great reverence for the divine as well as gentleness towards animals. He became a priest expert in religious ritual, but also devoted time to private worship and meditation in the loneliness of the windswept desert. At the age of thirty, traditionally for Iranians the time at which a man came into wisdom, Zoroaster had the first of many visions of the Wise Lord Ahura Mazda.

One spring morning Zoroaster rose early in a still dawn of delicate beauty. He went to the river to wash and collect water with which to mix the pressed *haoma* juice for the rituals of the *yasna*, or daily act of worship. As he emerged from the water he saw a vast and brightly shining figure on the bank who announced himself as Vohu Manah ("Good Purpose"). Vohu Manah led Zoroaster to a place awash with holy light, so bright that a man cast no shadow on the ground. Bathed in this thrilling radiance were six figures whom Zoroaster learned to be Ahura Mazda and five angels. They beckoned him forwards and announced that his learning would begin. From them he received instruction in the truth about the good creation and humans' role in the battle against evil. And they told Zoroaster that he would be a target for the forces of wickedness.

Zoroaster – Prophet or Trickster?

Seen by his followers as a great prophet, Zoroaster was cast in strikingly different lights by peoples of other lands and faiths. For some he encapsulated the mystery of eastern mysticism, while for others he proved a disruptive spiritual rival.

The Ancient Greeks regarded Zoroaster as the foremost of the Persian magi, priests expert in magic and steeped in ancient wisdom. They believed that the deeds of his life were lost in the mists of time, since, in an apparent misunderstanding of the Zoroastrian historical scheme, they placed him 6,000 years before Plato, who lived c.427–347BC. Tantalisingly, references survive to books by Zoroaster that were extant in the Greek world but have since disappeared.

A Zoroastrian fire altar on the reverse side of a Sasanian coin from the reign of King Ardashir I, AD224–242.

Early Christians tried to discredit Zoroaster, describing the prophet as a master of trickery and wicked spells. They said that his death came about when a furious spirit dispatched heavenly fire to destroy him. According to this account Zoroaster's deluded followers kept their master's ashes as a holy relic and worshipped the star that they believed had taken him into God's own Heaven. They explained the Greek version of his name as meaning "living star" (in Greek *zoro* is linked to the word for "life" and *aster* means "star"). The Persian, Zarathustra, on the other hand, means "he who seeks camels".

Zoroaster had seven further visions of Ahura Mazda before he began to share what he had learned with his fellow men. As he travelled around preaching, he attracted the restless forces of evil to him and demons tried many times to tempt him from the truth – but to no avail. According to some accounts it took Zoroaster ten years to convince anyone of the verity of his message. Leaving his homeland in order to make converts, the prophet was led by Ahura Mazda to attempt the conversion of King Vishtaspa, who was probably the ruler of Khorasmia, in Central Asia. At Vishtaspa's court were many learned scholars and magi expert in the dark secrets of magic. Zoroaster debated with them for three days while the king looked on. Vishtaspa initially felt a growing respect for this strange preacher who seemed to know exactly what he was thinking, but then he was given evidence that Zoroaster was a sorcerer who summoned the spirits of the dead.

Zoroaster was seized and shut up in a deep dungeon. Almost at once Vishtaspa's highly prized black stallion fell victim to a foul disease and its legs disappeared into its body. From his dungeon Zoroaster sent word that he could cure the horse, and would do so on four conditions: that Vishtaspa convert to the new religion, that the valorous prince Isfandiyar (see page 96) agree to fight on behalf of Zoroaster's faith, that the queen should also convert and, finally, that the king discover and reveal the names of the priests who had called Zoroaster a sorcerer. One by one Vishtaspa granted the conditions and the legs of his stallion re-emerged, as healthy and strong as before.

Then Vishtaspa begged to see himself sitting safely in Heaven. Instantly light filled the palace and three glorious immortals appeared in the very throne room. Fear drove the king and his followers to prostrate themselves, but the divine visitors assured them all of Ahura Mazda's good will and they were filled with joy. Many miracles later occurred: Vishtaspa saw himself in the glory of Heaven as he had wished, Prince Isfandiyar was granted invincible powers as a warrior, and the king's other son, Peshyotan, was made immortal.

Rock-relief showing the investiture of Ardashir I by Ahura Mazda, from Naqsh-i Rustam in Iran. Like all ancient Near Eastern kings, the Sasanians saw their line blessed by the highest god in the land.

An Eternal Flame

Vishtaspa proved an invaluable convert and with his backing Zoroaster's religion became a powerful force in the land. The prophet travelled far and wide preaching the word and many people memorized his lilting hymns and spread their master's message further.

At the age of seventy-seven Zoroaster was murdered while at worship – in some accounts as he performed a sacrifice in the temple. Curiously, Zoroastrian mythology does not give any further details of his death, but a colourful account of it was invented by early Christians seeking to demean the prophet (see box, page 54). Zoroaster's passing, however, was not a tragedy, for his life's work was done and the religion that he had been sent by Ahura Mazda to propagate – and which was to become such a powerful force in the Oriental world – was established for all time.

Forces of Good and Evil

Zoroaster believed that a battle was raging in the world and in the souls of men between the forces of good and evil. He identified two opposing spirits that had come into conflict at the beginning of time, behind whose figureheads stood a host of divinities, angels and, on the side of wickedness, demons. Men were Ahura Mazda's helpers in the war against evil, the defeat of which was the very purpose of creation.

A battle between the forces of Persia and Turan, from a late 16th-century edition of Firdowsi's *Shahnameh*. The conflicts between the two rival kingdoms were presented, in Zoroastrian tradition, as the very struggle between good and evil – the latter embodied by the northern foe.

Zoroaster understood Ahura Mazda as the source of all goodness and creator of all good things. According to the orthodox interpretation of Zoroaster's teaching, Ahura Mazda did not create evil – for the evil spirit existed from the beginning in opposition to goodness. The evil spirit was known as Angra Mainyu, although this is not used as a personal name in Zoroaster's *Gatha*.

Angra Mainyu sulked in a dark cavern. Tormented by the glorious light of Ahura Mazda's Heaven high above him, he resolved to destroy creation (see page 30). Later descriptions of the Wise Lord, from the Sasanian era (AD224–651), picture him on a heavenly throne, clad in a wondrous robe of blue that sparkles with points of light like stars in the night sky. For Angra Mainyu, however, there was nothing but darkness.

Dualism – the belief that good and evil have existed eternally and are in universal conflict – is generally identified as one of the key doctrines of Zoroastrianism. But at one point in the *Gatha* Zoroaster refers to the primeval spirits of good and evil as "twins", presupposing a father or mother, and some scholars have questioned whether he really was a dualist. According to this interpretation, it was the holy spirit of Ahura Mazda, Spenta Mainyu, who came into conflict with the evil spirit and not the Wise Lord, who existed before all other things. The conclusion is not that Ahura Mazda created evil: he simply gave issue to the two spirits, one of whom chose evil and the other good. An unorthodox form of Zoroastrianism named Zurvanism preached that good and evil were the twin offspring of a being, called Zurvan-i Akanarak, or "Infinite Time" (see box, page 58).

The Holy Immortals

In his glory Ahura Mazda created six offspring, the shining *Amesha Spenta*, or "Holy Immortals". They have abstract names and represent attributes of the Wise Lord and his creation. Through them *ashavan*, or righteous followers of the so-called Good Religion, can have access to these qualities. By means of the six Holy Immortals, Ahura Mazda brought forth the universe, which was viewed as seven distinct creations in the Iranian tradition. Each creation was protected by either Ahura Mazda or one of his six Immortals.

The most important of the Immortals was Vohu Manah who had led Zoroaster into the divine presence at the time of the prophet's first vision (see page 54). He was protector of the sustaining cow. In some texts he is said to be the eldest of the Holy Immortals and to sit at the right hand of Ahura Mazda – as Christians later told of Jesus Christ. Asha Vahishta ("Best Righteousness") was protector of the sacred fire. As personification of *asha* itself, he was a being of breathtaking beauty and was a resolute enemy of disease and death on Earth.

Righteous Warriors

The good-willed gods of the pagan Iranians lived on in Zoroastrianism as the yazata ("Worshipful Ones"). They were created by the Holy Immortals and ranked beneath them in the divine hierarchy.

The *yazata* were warriors in the ceaseless battle against evil. The most important was Mithra, *yazata* of loyalty, who was linked to the sun and who judged men at the death of their physical bodies. Apam Napat, another of the ancient guardians of *asha*, was *yazata* of honesty and oaths. Ashi was associated with fortune, Haoma with the sacred plant, while Atar remained linked with fire. Other pagan gods lived on too: Verethragna as *yazata* of victory, and Vayu as patron of wind and life's breath.

Sraosha was *yazata* of obedience, a virtue that was believed to be a mighty force against evil. In the sacred rituals he took the form of the worshippers' prayers, and carried their petitions to Heaven. He was an armed warrior who patrolled the Earth at night when demons were at their most powerful. His special enemy was the demon Aeshma ("Fury"). Sraosha lived in a hall with

1,000 pillars, lit by twinkling stars at the very top of Mount Haraiti. He rode in a chariot hauled by snorting snow-white steeds shod with glittering gold.

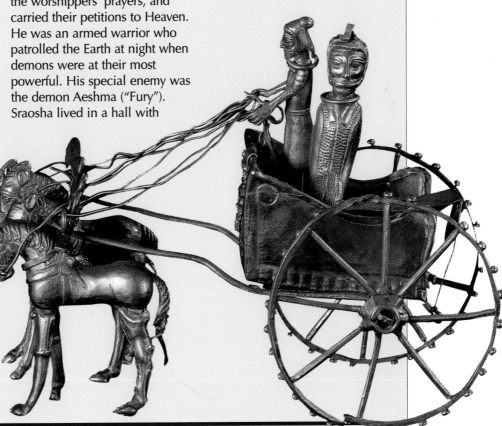

The *yazata* Sraosha rode in a chariot; this gold one is from the Oxus treasure, c.5th–4th century BC.

A Doubtful Heresy

Zurvanism was a significant movement within the Zoroastrian faith in the Sasanian period (AD 224–651). It taught that the spirits of good and evil were twin offspring of an absolute being: Zurvan-i Akanarak ("Infinite Time").

Scholars are unsure both of the date when Zurvanism emerged and its exact nature because no Zurvanite literature has survived. Some idea of its beliefs, however, has been deduced from various Zoroastrian and non-Persian accounts.

Zurvan is described as living entirely alone until he performed a 1,000-year religious sacrifice in an attempt to create a son. When no child appeared he began to doubt whether the sacrifice would ever work – but from that doubt two children were born within him: Ohrmazd and Ahriman. Zurvan pledged to give power over the later creation to whichever son appeared first. Maddened by the desire for power, Ahriman tore his way out of Zurvan and presented himself as Ohrmazd. But Zurvan was not fooled and when Ohrmazd finally emerged Zurvan at once gave him the barsom twigs or grasses that Persian priests used in their rituals.

Ohrmazd created Heaven and Earth, and Ahriman made all bad things. Zurvan had to keep his promise and gave the wicked Ahriman power over the Earth for 9,000 years, at the end of which good would be restored. The Zurvanite myth therefore taught that the full range of good and evil, light and dark, was to be found in potential form in the unity of the primeval god – for evil grew from a moment of divine doubt.

A silver figurine of a king, c.5th–4th century BC. He is holding sacred barsom twigs like those that Zurvan gave to Ohrmazd.

Spenta Armaiti ("Holy Devotion"), protector of the Earth, was a fair daughter of the Wise Lord and was imagined sitting at his left hand. Khshathra Vairya ("Desirable Dominion") was responsible for the security of the overarching sky, Haurvatat ("Health" or "Well-being") was guardian of water and Ameretat ("Long Life") overseer of plants. Ahura Mazda himself kept watch over the seventh creation, humankind. The daily *yasna* was understood to sustain these creations and honoured the Holy Immortals through their identifications with them.

Ahura Mazda and the Holy Immortals were both many and one. The Wise Lord was sometimes seen as the father of the Immortals; at others he was said to have mixed himself with them. One interpretation was that the Immortals were like many torches lit from a single flame. Ahura Mazda and the Immortals had a single purpose and a collective consciousness. In later Zoroastrian texts, however, the Immortals were seen less as aspects of Ahura Mazda and more as independent personal gods or angels. They were pictured on towering thrones of gold, and were said to inhabit a heaven named the House of Song. This image later greatly influenced the picture of angels and archangels in Christianity. From the Holy Immortals emerged other sacred beings known as the *yazata* or "Worshipful Ones" who were surviving forms of some of the gods of the pagan Indo-Iranians (see box, page 57).

Soldiers of Darkness

In the first days, when the good spirit chose benevolence, the evil spirit chose wickedness – and their choices resulted in the good and evil creations respectively. The followers of *druj* were constantly at war with the good creation.

In later literature the evil spirit Angra Mainyu, or Ahriman, was said to live in a darkly shadowed crater in the utmost north – traditionally the place from which demons emerged. He could take the form of a supple and canny youth, a wily snake or a darting lizard. He created all that was evil in direct opposition to goodness: ugliness to counteract beauty, disease to undermine health, death to end life.

Zoroaster condemned worship of the warlike divinities in the pagan pantheon, for he associated them with cattle-rustling Aryan raiders and with ritual animal sacrifice. From the time when the pagan Iranians had mixed with the Aryan nomads before their migration to Iran and India, they had worshipped two types of divinity, an ethical god and a martial one. Originally the names *daeva* and *ahura* – or *deva* and *asura* – were titles for gods, but Zoroaster restricted the use of *daeva* to the warlike deities. He said the *daeva* had been misled by the evil spirit and had chosen wickedness, and so they were numbered among the demons. Curiously, in India and Iran the two titles came to have opposite meanings: in Zoroastrianism *ahura* were worshipped and *daeva* condemned, while in India after around 1000BC *asura* became a title for demons and *deva* a name for gods. The cult of some martial gods survived in India too, most notably that of Indra, who was worshipped by the Indian Aryans as the storm god and a divine warrior. In Zoroastrianism, however, he was one of the chief demons.

Other demons of Zoroastrianism were Sauru, bringer of anarchy and patron of drunkenness; strutting Naonhaithyeh, the source of arrogance; and Aka Manah, the embodiment of evil. The demon Aeshma ("Fury"), with a ravening thirst for violence and conflict, took pleasure in provoking arguments both among righteous *ashavan* and between demons. Those on Earth who neglected their appearance and who fell under the spell of intoxicants were particularly at risk from Aeshma.

The bloodthirsty, three-headed dragon Azhi Dahaka was one of a class of lesser demons sometimes named *druj* from the term for falsehood. Azhi Dahaka longed to strip the Earth of life. His body was a heaving mound of scorpions, lizards and other foul, poison-tongued insects.

Part of a bronze horse bit in the form of a human-headed beast, from Luristan, western Iran, *c.*800–700BC. Zoroaster condemned the pagans' warlike deities, linking them with the nomadic Aryan raiders who sowed destruction wherever they rode.

These fiendish beasts lurked within his ever-creeping skin, and there were enough to cover the entire Earth if he should ever burst open. In some traditions he became the serpent-shouldered King Zahak (see page 42); another myth told how he was finally defeated by the brave warrior Thraetaona and imprisoned in Mount Demavand.

Nasu represented bodily corruption and decay and brought infection wherever he went. Jahi was a lithe-bodied female who sought to seduce men and bring them to their ruin, while other demons included abstractions such as jealousy and wrong-mindedness.

59

Tales of Creation

The evil one Angra Mainyu rose up from his home in the lower darkness to attack Ahura Mazda. The Wise Lord at once offered peace if his opponent would recognize and praise goodness, but the evil spirit thirsted for destruction and rejected the offer, promising to attack good in all its forms wherever he found it.

Ahura Mazda realized that evil might eventually pollute goodness if it was allowed to oppose him for all time, so he proposed that the battle between them should be for a fixed period only. Angra Mainyu, in whom intelligence had been overcome by ignorance and the lust for violence, impulsively agreed. In that moment he doomed himself to final defeat, for at the end of the allotted period good will dispatch evil once and for all.

Then Ahura Mazda unleashed the auspicious words of an ancient Zoroastrian prayer, the *Ahuna Vairya*, in which the Wise Lord is celebrated as the master of *asha* as well as the source of life and all benevolent things. Zoroastrians believe that the

A miniature painting of a woman reclining, by Mir Afzal Tumi, *c*.1645. Angra Mainyu hoped that his seductress Jahi would turn men away from the service of their creator, Ahura Mazda.

prayer contains the very essence of their faith and say that reciting it surpasses any other form of worship. When the Wise Lord used the sacred words for the first time, they resounded in all places and Angra Mainyu trembled with rage and fear, for he understood finally that evil would never be a match for good. He fell away into the dark chasm of his first awakening, and lay there as if dead for 3,000 years.

The Resurgence of Evil

The good creation took form through the power of Ahura Mazda. From the bright purity of the light in which he existed he made the universe in its spiritual aspect – called *menog* or "immaterial" in Pahlavi; then he fashioned the *getig* ("material") form of creation. First he made the Holy Immortals and through them the worshipful *yazata*. Then he formed the world, which took a shape almost identical to that described in ancient Indo-Iranian creation myths (see page 28). He built the sturdy stone shell that enclosed all things, its top half forming the sky and the bottom half filled with sweet waters. On the surface he launched the floating Earth. In the centre of the Earth, he formed a strong and sturdy tree, a broad-shouldered ox and the primeval man Gayomartan (called Gayomard in Pahlavi and Kiyumars in the *Shahnameh*). No bark or pricking thorn grew on the tree, for all things took their most perfect form: the ox's skin was of an unblemished white and Gayomartan's metal body, which in some accounts was said to be as wide as it was tall, shone brilliantly like the sun. The Earth was perfectly flat and in the sky the sun always sat high at its noon zenith.

By this time Angra Mainyu had revived from his despair. As life stirred again within him, he shook with a monstrous, perverted form of the Wise Lord's creative power and a host of wicked demons emerged from his belly. Among them was narrow-waisted Jahi, the delicately formed seductress. She knelt close to her evil master whispering of her plans to infect all things with evil and

It was said that the arid deserts of Persia, such as this one near Yazd, were created by the evil one, Angra Mainyu.

to heap misery on the sturdy ox and righteous Gayomartan. Pleased with her words, Angra Mainyu himself dallied and flirted with her, leading her on with the tantalizing promise that she would have the power to seduce men from their destiny as servants of the Wise Lord.

Then from his dark pit Angra Mainyu saw the good creation, vibrant with light, and hurled himself into attack. With the demon army at his back he broke through the lower half of the encompassing stone shell and lunged upwards through the waters, fouling them with bitter salt. The whole of the good creation shook before his onslaught, and the evil spirit and his demons attacked every good thing they saw.

On Earth Angra Mainyu made the wind-blasted deserts that are enemies of plant and animal life, and dreamt up the whirlwind and the sandstorm to be tools of his chaotic intent. He gouged holes in the flat surface of the fruitful earth to make plunging valleys and used the soil to pile up towering, barren mountain peaks. He toppled the sun from its ideal place at the top of the sky, poisoned the primeval plant and brutally slew the ox. He even dirtied the pure and sacred fire with swirling smoke. Gayomartan resisted the

61

forces of evil for thirty years since this had been ordained by Ahura Mazda. At the end of this time the *yazata* grappled with demons throughout the material universe for ninety days, but then evil finally appeared to triumph – Gayomartan succumbed to the malicious force and died.

Ahura Mazda's creation had been pure and wholly good, but Angra Mainyu defiled it with the myriad shapes of physical and moral evil. By Zoroastrian tradition it is an act of great wickedness to deny the essential goodness of the material world, and Zoroastrians feel great reverence for physical things, especially in their purest forms such as fire or water. They believe that evil is a spiritual force that usually cannot take a physical form – although pollution and some creatures are said to be evil (see page 64).

The Army of Good Men

Now Angra Mainyu surveyed his handiwork and a grim pleasure flooded through him. He turned his face to the dark place he called home, but then was stopped in his tracks. Before him towered the spirit of the sky, dressed in heavy armour and bristling with weapons, at the head of a heavenly host of the *fravashi* or celestial souls of men. The *fravashi* had elected to help Ahura Mazda in the battle against wickedness.

The evil one turned back but saw that he was trapped – for now the stone shell that arched over and under the Earth appeared to be like the thick walls of a prison and, despite his best efforts, he was unable to release himself. The Wise Lord is therefore said to have made the universe in order to combat evil. Some accounts suggest that his purpose was to protect himself from the attacks of Angra Mainyu. According to this interpretation, the evil spirit is pictured as a prisoner because his malicious intent is trapped in the material world and so he is unable to harm Ahura Mazda.

Now the forces of good set to work. Ameretat, the *Amesha Spenta* revered as the protector of plants, crushed the primeval tree like a priest pounding the juice out of a *haoma* plant for the *yasna* ritual, then sent rains and winds to carry its essence through the world. Plants sprang up everywhere. From the prostrate body of the slaughtered ox sprang nourishing grains and healing herbs. Its semen rose to the ever watchful moon, where it was purified and gave life to herd upon herd of mild-mannered cattle, as well as all other animals. Gayomartan's semen meanwhile was cleansed by the sun and found issue in generations of men and women; humankind, like the rest of the good creation, was made out of and for the struggle of good against evil. In another version Gayomartan's metal body and semen passed into the earth, creating rich veins of minerals and metals and the first humans, who grew in the form of a plant (see box opposite).

In the traditional Indo-Iranian creation stories, the gods had killed the first plant, ox and man as a propitious sacrifice and their action resulted in the abundance of life on Earth (see page 29). But the reworked Zoroastrian account made the sacrifice of the primeval forms of life an act of evil that was only turned to good by the *Amesha Spenta* and other forces of *asha*.

A pharmacist prepares drugs in a scene from a 13th-century Persian manuscript of Dioscorides's *Materia Medica*. The creation of healing herbs was a crucial step towards confounding the corrupting designs of Angra Mainyu.

Cycles of History

According to Zoroastrianism, history will last for 12,000 years, divided into four spells of three millennia. For the pagan Indo-Iranians and their Zoroastrian descendants, as for many other cultures, the number three and its compounds are highly auspicious. In this historical scheme, the first 3,000 years witnessed the creation of the *menog,* or spiritual creation, and corresponded to the time when the evil spirit lay sunk in despair in his filthy lair. The next 3,000 saw the establishment of the *getig* physical universe (see page 61). At the beginning of the third period of time, Angra Mainyu launched an attack on the good creation, and the following stage of history saw the eventual mingling of good and evil in the universe. Zoroaster's glorious birth marked the end of this period and ushered in the final three millennia, in which the hostile spirit will at last be dispatched and good will finally triumph (see page 69).

The Coming of Mortals

The life of the primeval man Gayomartan was short, but years later bore fruit in a plant from which the first mortal men and women emerged to populate the world.

The moment Gayomartan was slain, his semen passed into the earth. For forty years the sun shone brightly on that same spot and eventually a rhubarb plant forced its way from the soil. The plant's stalks and leaves then became the bodies and limbs of a man and woman, Mashya and Mashyanag, who were father and mother of the ten races of humankind.

The human couple soon broke free of the plant's roots to walk upon the Earth. Ahura Mazda then explained to them that they should always seek good and avoid evil. But the forces of wickedness rushed in on Mashya and Mashyanag, and in their delusion the first man and woman saw the world as a harsh and unwelcoming place and declared it to be the creation of the evil spirit. It was the first and greatest of all sins, a sacrilegious denial of Ahura Mazda's handiwork.

Mashya and Mashyanag lost their way and strayed far from the path of *asha* that Ahura Mazda had laid out for them. Although they made ritual sacrifices and did not shrink from virtuous labour, they were unable to escape the evil spell cast over them by Angra Mainyu. They even lost their desire to increase the human population through joyful sexual union. For fifty sterile years they lived in the world without producing offspring. Finally, however, Mashyanag gave birth to a pair of twins.

But instead of loving and protecting their firstborn, Mashya and Mashyanag butchered and ate them. At that time the flesh of young children tasted sweet – so Ahura Mazda took that delicate flavour away.

Many years later Mashya and Mashyanag produced another set of twins, who grew into strong, healthy adults. They were the parents of the tribes of Iran, and through them of the entire human race.

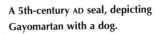

A 5th-century AD seal, depicting Gayomartan with a dog.

63

The Division of Animals

Orthodox Zoroastrians believe that evil cannot take physical form because Ahura Mazda's material creation is entirely good. Nevertheless they have traditionally avoided some creatures that they associate with evil while revering others that they believe are especially beneficent.

A religious document from the Sasanians (AD224–651) describes how Ahura Mazda understood that some powerful forms of evil would be more dangerous in a spiritual state than they would be if they could be seen – so he gave them physical form. This is how Zoroastrians explain the existence of some entirely evil creatures within his benevolent creation.

Zoroastrians see death as an evil force that pollutes creation and hold strong beliefs about the power of purity and cleanliness as a positive force. For instance, they teach that anything expelled or removed from the human body – excrement, cut hair, clipped nails, even exhaled breath – is dead and impure. Animals and insects commonly associated with death and dirt are ranked among the evil creatures, or *khrafstra*. Foremost among them is the fly, but beetles, swarming wasps, ants and rats are also associated with Angra Mainyu.

The dangerously seductive female demons, or *pairaka*, appear as sleek, bright-eyed rats. Another demonic female spirit named Naush takes the appearance of a mottled fly said to ride the ill-omened winds from the north, where Zoroastrians traditionally believed that evil had its home. When a soul departs from its physical body, she flies down at once and alights on the corpse.

To the Zoroastrian mind, ugly creatures such as toads or lizards offend against the well-proportioned beauty of the good creation; they are easily explained as one of the physical forms that Ahura Mazda gave to evil to limit its power. A frog is cast as the enemy of the abundant creation, for it is said to gnaw at the roots of the Tree of Many Seeds that towers high into the sky above the cosmic ocean of Vourukasha (see page 29).

The silent snake and the scorpion, whose attacks can end a man's life, are also feared and reviled as evil, as in the past were the shaggy-maned lions that at one time prowled the Iranian plateau and haunted the dreams of cross-country travellers. Zoroastrians also distrust domestic cats because of their family link to beasts of prey.

Some animals on the other hand are seen as divinely ordained allies of humans in the long battle against evil. Foremost among these are the cow and the dog. The latter – faithful, obedient and warm-hearted – embodies some of the essential qualities that the Wise Lord gave his people, and to which the followers of righteousness should aspire. Certain dogs are said to have wonderful powers. The foul fly-demoness Naush can be driven away by a dog with a yellow coat and six eyes or a yellow-eared white dog. For the pagan Indo-Iranian settlers and their descendants cattle were a revered symbol for the whole of the Wise Lord's

A copper and silver inlaid mace head in the form of a lion, from Khorasan in northeast Persia, c.11th–12th century.

good and generous creation. The cow, which provided food in the form of its flesh and milk, fuel in its dung, and clothing in its skin, was central to their very survival. Even its urine was of benefit since it functioned as a powerful cleaner because of the large amount of ammonia that it contains.

It was used to purify vessels before the *yasna* ritual. Cattle in the form of the ox came to stand for the whole of the animal kingdom in creation myths, while sacred bulls are still kept by Parsis in their temples: hairs from the animals' tails are used to make a filter for straining *haoma* liquid.

Mythical Beasts

A menagerie of wonderful creatures inhabited the imaginary world of Zoroastrianism. In the very highest branches of the Tree of Many Seeds sat the Saena – a winged beast, half bird and half dog, who by raising itself up and flapping its wings created a wind that carried the seeds far and wide.

In Pahlavi the bird was called Senmurv and it may have been the source for Simurgh, another winged creature known from later traditions (see page 108). It was sometimes said to have a nest in the tree and to suckle its offspring there like a dog.

Through the waves that lapped around the base of the Tree of Many Seeds swam the *kar*, the ten magnificent fish who tirelessly circled to drive away the enemies of *asha* such as the lizard whose task was to try to bite the tree's roots (see page 29). A magnificent ass with brilliant white skin also protected the tree. It had the auspicious number of nine mouths, six eyes and three legs; a glittering golden horn protruded from its forehead.

Another bird, the Chamrush, helped to distribute the seeds from the tree. It was traditionally a fierce opponent of Persia's enemies and myths told how it would swoop down from a sun-drenched sky to attack them with its sharp beak.

Stories of Zoroaster's life recount how the Karshiptar, a strong-winged bird, flew far and wide carrying the prophet's teachings to all who would listen. There was also the holy owl Ashozushta, who knew prayers that could vanquish demons.

But not all Zoroastrianism's fantastical creatures were defenders of the faith, for some were part of

the demon army of *druj* created by Angra Mainyu. The most powerful of the demonic beasts was Azhi Dahaka, a six-eyed dragon with three heads and three fiery mouths (see page 34).

Goblet decorated with mythological monsters, from northwest Iran, *c.*1200BC. It is made out of electrum, an alloy of gold and silver used in ancient times.

65

Visions of the Afterlife

After death, Zoroastrians hold that all men and women are judged for their conduct on Earth. The soul may then pass to one of three places according to the righteousness of the life it has led. Such beliefs had ancient pagan roots – but with Zoroaster's influence the visions of punishment and eternal joy were to influence many future religions.

For the first three nights after death, the soul is stricken with sadness at having been separated from its physical home and hovers close to the place in which the body is laid to rest. It ponders over the life it has lived, on the first night recalling words, on the second thoughts and on the third actions. Demons swarm about, eager to inflict harm, but the soul, if fortunate, is protected by the prayers and rituals of relatives on Earth.

At dawn on the fourth day the soul begins its long journey towards judgement. It is transported into the presence of the worshipful beings Mithra, Sraosha and Rashnu. They use scales to weigh up good and evil in the individual's past thoughts, words and deeds on Earth. Here the souls of all people are judged on exactly the same basis – whether they be rich or poor, priest or farmer. If the balance tips in favour of good rather than evil, the soul is touched by a sweet and gentle breeze and looks up to see a bright-skinned maiden of surpassing beauty. In a voice vibrant with joy, she introduces herself as the pure conscience of the righteous soul. But if the balance tips in favour of evil, then the soul sees an ugly crone with rotting flesh, foul breath and a pock-marked face: the shape of a diseased, unused conscience.

Both good and evil souls come to a barrier: the Bridge of Chinvat. To the good it appears as a wide and easy way that is thronged with the spiritual shapes of the righteous *yazata* and leads happily to Heaven. But the wicked are confronted with a thin ledge like a mountain ridge from which rocks and scree plunge vertiginously away on both sides. They only manage to cross halfway before they fall off, tumbling in the embrace of the foul hag screaming down to Hell. There are a few souls, however, for whom the scales of judgement are balanced between good and evil, and they are led away to a third place – Misvan Gatu ("Place of the Mixed Ones"), also known as *hamestagan*.

In Zoroastrian mythology, Heaven and Hell are minutely imagined places, with physical locations – Heaven above, in or beyond the light-drenched sky; Hell below, in a colourless underworld. The image of the afterlife was closely based on the picture of life after death held by the Zoroastrians' ancestors among the Indo-Iranian nomads. They too believed that the soul must remain on Earth for three nights after death and that happy souls seeking paradise had to pass across the Bridge of Chinvat. But in their imagination only people of worldly importance could reach Heaven; all the poor, and probably all women, went to the world of the dead ruled by the primeval king, Yima.

Heaven and Hell are not eternal, for Zoroastrians believe that all men and women are judged twice for their conduct on Earth: once after the death of the physical body, and then at the end of history when the battle against evil has been won. Ahura Mazda does not condemn sinners to endless suffering, but does purge them of wrong-doing. All men and women are part of the good creation and are destined to share with Ahura Mazda in the rejoicing that will follow the final defeat of evil.

The Vision of Viraf

In one story, the faithful *ashavan* Viraf was rewarded for his righteousness with a vision of the joys of Heaven and the sufferings of the accursed in Hell.

The *yazata* of obedience, Sraosha, led Viraf across the Bridge of Chinvat to the plains of Heaven where he saw the souls of righteous men and women glittering like stars in the sky. He came into the very presence of Ahura Mazda where he witnessed the joyous *ashavan* of all types and classes including virtuous and loyal wives, farmers, craftsmen and those who honoured peace. They lived in delight with their lord among soft cushions on beautiful carpets of the most majestic colours.

Viraf's guide through Hell was a hideous old crone. With her he witnessed dreadful suffering in a place where shadows were so thick a man could grasp them. For these poor souls time seemed to pass tortuously slowly and their punishments appeared to last indefinitely.

Once judged by the three worshipful beings, the soul either looks towards the beneficent maiden with her welcoming arms outstretched, or into the hideous face of the crone who brings damnation for those who spurned the righteous path during their life on Earth.

Evil Vanquished

Zoroaster's life and teaching ushered in the fourth and final stage of history. The 3,000 years after his death were to see an epic struggle between virtue and wickedness. This epoch was itself divided into four eras. In the golden time, Zoroaster experienced his revelation of the Good Religion; in the silver he converted Vishtaspa. The steel period was that of the Sasanians, while in the final age of iron evil would seem to be triumphant.

By tradition Zoroaster experienced a vision of the resurgence of evil: he saw an unruly horde of unkempt demons assault Persia. He watched as earthquakes and droughts devastated the crops while the poor starved; in the heavens, sun and moon were dimmed. The vision struck awe into the heart of the prophet and he begged to be spared having to live through this dread age. But hope would return, he learned, when a cascade of brilliant stars was seen in the blue heavens – for it was a sign that a prince had been born who would drive evil from the land before the birth of a Heaven-sent saviour.

The First Victories of Good

The Wise Lord decreed that three saviours should appear on Earth to help virtue in its perilous struggle with wickedness in the age of iron. Each of these warriors would be born of a pure-hearted virgin but would also be a son of Zoroaster. By wondrous occurrence the prophet's semen was stored in a Persian lake of crystal waters where, at the appointed time, the chosen maiden would be moved to bathe. Zoroaster's seed, floating free in the waters, would cause her to conceive a holy child.

A Sasanian king fends off lions in a design on a silver dish, c.5th century AD. Zoroaster believed that humankind had to battle the designs of evil right up to the very final age of history.

The first saviour was Aushedar and during his lifetime the power of evil would begin to wane. When he attained thirty, the age of wisdom, the sun would for ten days resume its ideal noon position and conflict in the world would die away for three years. But then evil would strike back.

In the time of the second saviour, Aushedar-mah, good would grow twice as strong as before. The sun would stop in its noon position for twenty days rather than ten, while peace and prosperity would wash over the world for six years instead of three. Serpents and many other *khrafstra* would be seen no more. Men and women would turn away from eating animal flesh and choose to subsist on the bountiful fruits of the Earth, drinking pure sweet water in place of milk or wine. But then the foul dragon Azhi Dahaka would burst from the side of Mount Demavand where it had been imprisoned by Thraetaona (see page 44). Only after a time of devastation would mighty Keresaspa (see page 46) finally come back to life and dispatch Azhi Dahaka once and for all.

The third saviour, Soshyant, would preside over the final defeat of evil and the restoration of the good creation to its perfect state. He would raise the bodies of the dead and reunite them with their souls before calling all to a great Last Judgement. On that day, separating virtuous from wicked would be as easy as choosing white sheep or black. The good would proceed to Heaven and the evil to Hell for three days and nights. Creation would be purged of evil as the worshipful *yazata* fought their opponents among the demon army.

Punishment in Hell would restore the wicked to righteousness. Then the *yazata* of healing, Airyaman, would melt the metal in the mountains – creating a molten sheet like the sea of lava that pours from an angry volcano. The molten metal would sweep across creation, smoothing away the mountains and valleys to restore the Earth to its original perfect flatness. Men and women would pass through it but because they were now righteous it would seem to them like a gentle bath of milk. The wicked demons would be killed and Angra Mainyu finally destroyed.

A prince is entertained in the countryside, in an opaque watercolour from Isfahan, *c.*1650. Such scenes recall the Zoroastrian vision of the end of time when people will live in the bright and glorious light of Ahura Mazda's beautiful creation.

Then Soshyant would perform an auspicious sacrifice, slaughtering the heavenly ox Srishok. Soshyant would mix a wondrous drink with the fat of the ox and the fruit of the white Hom, the tree that grew in the Vourukasha sea. The drink would make all men and women immortal in body and soul, perfectly uniting matter and spirit as Ahura Mazda had originally intended. Death would be annihilated. The *Amesha Spenta*, the worshipful *yazata*, men and women would live together with Ahura Mazda in perfect contentment on Earth, surrounded by gentle light in an abundance of plants and sweetly scented flowers.

PATTERNS OF PERFECTION

Intricate patterns are a hallmark of Persian art, from painting and pottery to architecture and calligraphy. Such ornamentation, however, is much more than superficial decoration: it reflects a search for order amid chaos and a belief in transcending the objective world through design – transporting the viewer beyond the bounds of immediate experience into the presence of the divine.

Artistic reflections of the rhythmic multiplicity of the creation first flowered with the coming of Islam, when the written word displaced oral poetic forms and calligraphy was elevated to a place of prime importance, led by illustrated manuscripts and the Koran. The fluid forms of such texts found their decorative equivalents in the complex floral and geometrical designs which characterize the masterpieces of Islamic art. Thus the facades of mosques and the arabesques of carpets, tiles and texts all reflect the essential harmony at the heart of the universe and bear witness to a powerful belief that unifies aesthetic and spiritual convictions.

Left: Interior decoration helped to create a mood of perfect equilibrium by denying the eye one particular point on which to focus. The multiple surfaces on the ceiling of the Masjed-e Emam, built in Isfahan in 1638, seem to dissolve, suggesting the transient nature of both earthly structures and human life.

Left: This 15th-century Koranic inscription shows how closely calligraphy merges with floral and geometric forms. Such texts were not always legible, however, for the more ornate inscriptions were designed to evoke a divine presence rather than to be read.

Right: The mix of geometric and floral patterns occurs again on this ancient rug from northwest Persia. Many styles, particularly those used in carpets, have their origins in designs which pre-date the coming of Islam. Some scholars have even suggested that motifs survive which could be up to 3,000 years old.

Left: The Masjed-e Jameh, in Isfahan, a mosque and a museum of Islamic architecture, mixes influences from the pre-Islamic Sasanian period to the 18th century. The striking tilework and calligraphy hide the essential simplicity of the mosque itself, which employs an architectural form derived from Parthian palaces. All the elements of the building, however, are unified by the elaborate ornamentation that gives Islamic architecture its unique quality. Colours provide additional symbolism, with the dominant blue and green suggesting water and cultivation, evidence of God's infinite mercy.

THE EPIC OF THE KINGS

By far the best-known source of Persian legend is the country's national epic, the *Shahnameh*, or "Book of Kings". Written by the poet Firdowsi at the turn of the tenth and eleventh centuries, it tells the story of Iran all the way from the Creation to the Arab conquest and the coming of Islam in AD642. The book occupies an extraordinary position in national life; even today, there are traditional story-tellers who can recount large parts of it from memory, and Iranians of all classes and from all walks of life know individual passages by heart.

Firdowsi came from the Persian landowner class and lived in Tus, in eastern Iran. He earned just enough from the rents on his various properties to devote his time to writing poetry. The *Shahnameh* was his life's work and it took him more than twenty-five years to complete. He may have originally hoped to dedicate it to the Samanid kings of eastern Iran who consciously set out to revive the nation's past glories, but by the time that he had finished it they had been overthrown by the Turkish Ghaznavid dynasty. Eager to earn a suitable dowry for his daughter, the poet took the poem to the dynasty's founder Mahmud of Ghazneh, a celebrated patron of the arts, but was treated unjustly; having been promised 60,000 gold coins for his efforts, he was in fact fobbed off with the same sum in silver. He left in anger, and subsequently composed a bitter satire on the ruler he thought had cheated him.

In writing the *Shahnameh*, Firdowsi drew on prose chronicles whose original sources stretched back to the early days of Persian history. He also knew the verses of an earlier poet, named Daqiqi, who had started setting these accounts in rhyme, only to be murdered after completing just a few thousand lines. Firdowsi was able to complete the task, recounting the deeds both of legendary early rulers who supposedly had reigned for hundreds of years and of later kings of dynasties for which reasonably accurate historical records had survived.

By the time he finally laid down his pen, he had composed an epic of some 50,000 couplets, or double verses, and had created for future generations a panorama of heroes and champions that itself became part of the national heritage it set out to portray.

Above: A royal seal from the Sasanian dynasty (AD224–651). The greatest of all their kings, Khusrow II, is mentioned in the epic poem the *Shahnameh.*

Opposite: The ruins of a medieval fort at Izad Khast in Fars province. Warfare was at the heart of Firdowsi's *Shahnameh.* The wars between Iran and Turan were mythical, but the tales of the Sasanian kings that formed the latter part of the epic were based on historical fact.

Zal the White-Haired Prince

Zal was a strong and healthy baby and the son of a king – yet one odd feature in his appearance caused his father cruelly to abandon him. But the Simurgh, that strange bird of Persian mythology, ensured the child survived to fulfil his, and his country's, destiny.

Zal, the white-haired child, is returned to his father, the king of Zabulestan, by the mythological bird, the Simurgh; from the *Shahnameh* of Mohammed Juki, *c.*1440. The strange appearance of the child led the king to denounce him as a demon. But Zal was later to father Persia's greatest hero, Rustam.

Sam, king of Zabulestan, was a famous warrior and one of the bravest tributary rulers of Manuchihr, undisputed King of Kings of all the Persians. Sam's reputation spread far and wide and he had everything anyone could wish for. Deep within his soul, however, he was troubled: for he longed for a son to succeed him. He was, therefore, more than usually delighted when word reached him that his wife was expecting a child. Yet when the long-awaited day of the birth came, no one rushed to tell him the happy news. For the baby, though well formed in every other way, had an oddity: his hair was as white as an old man's.

When an old nurse eventually found the courage to inform the king, his wife's worst fears were confirmed. Calling the baby a monster and the son of demons, he gave orders that it should be taken into the wilderness of the Alburz Mountains and abandoned on the barren slopes.

So the baby boy was left out in the heat of the sun, with only thorns for a cradle and the bare ground as a nurse. His cries soon attracted the attention of the Simurgh, the mighty bird of Persian legend, whose eyrie was on the range's topmost peak. Swooping down, it snatched up the crying child and carried him off to feed its own young. But the fledgelings would have none of this strange new addition to their diet, and soon pity stirred in the heart of the mother bird. Moved by the baby's cries, it decided to raise the human foundling itself as part of its brood. Before long it was feeding him the tenderest morsels it brought back to the nest.

Time passed, and the infant grew up to be a strong and handsome young man. Then one day a caravan passed over the mountains. The merchants were astonished to see, running wild among the peaks, a youth with the build of an athlete but with waist-length white hair. Word of the wonder spread throughout the district, and soon reached Sam in his palace. At once he realized that the strange figure could only be his long-lost son, who had somehow survived in the wilderness.

The old king determined to go at once to the mountains to find him. Seeing the royal party wending its way through the foothills, the Simurgh – who had magical wisdom as well as the power of speech – knew at once who its chief must be. It went to its human charge and bade him a sad farewell, telling him that at last the time had come for him to return to the world of men. But it would never forget him, it added, and would always come to him if he was in need; and it gave him a feather from its own breast, telling him to burn it if he required help. Then, lifting him in its claws, it soared down the mountainside to deposit him at the monarch's feet.

The king looked the boy over and realized that he was indeed his son – for here he stood, in every way fit to rule. Sam now bitterly repented his earlier cruelty, and with tears in his eyes begged the boy's forgiveness. And he gave him the name Zal – one that came to strike fear into the hearts of Iran's enemies. Yet even so it would eventually pale before that of the youth's own offspring, for in time he was to become the father of Rustam, the greatest of all the heroes of Iran.

The Triumph of Love

Zal's love for the daughter of a neighbouring ruler provided the Shahnameh with one of its most passionate romantic idylls.

Rudabeh was as beautiful as Zal was handsome and strong, and the two fell in love with each other by report before they ever met. But meeting was not easy. Rudabeh's father was the king of the border state of Kabulestan, and although he accepted the supreme authority of the Iranian King of Kings just as Sam did, he did so at best unwillingly. Worse, he was of the lineage of serpent-shouldered Zahak, the most hated of all Iran's early kings (see page 42).

So when Zal visited Kabulestan, he chose to pitch his tents across the river from Mehrab's capital rather than accept the ruler's proffered hospitality. Rudabeh was sequestered in the women's quarters of her father's palace, and etiquette would not allow Zal to request an introduction.

Eventually it was five of the princess's maids in waiting who found a way to break the deadlock. They went to relax on the riverbank in full view of the royal party opposite. Seeing a chance to break the ice, Zal snatched up his bow and brought down a passing bird that fell close to the spot where they were sitting. The prince then sent attendants to retrieve the game, telling them to engage the girls in conversation. Soon the two groups were each singing the praises of their respective employers. Zal took the opportunity to send presents of jewels for the princess, and a secret rendezvous was arranged.

The two fell head over heels in love with one another as soon as they met. At first their parents opposed the match, but their disapproval was swept away by the force of their passion. And so the pair were married among public rejoicing, and all the witnesses agreed that no more beautiful couple had ever graced a throne.

Zal wooed Rudabeh with jewels he sent via serving maids, before he ever met her. This gold brooch, inlaid with sapphire, dates from the 12th century.

The Boyhood of Rustam

For strength and valour no hero could match Rustam, the Persian Herakles. Even in childhood his great strength was evident – as an adult it was unsurpassed. Yet his birth was a difficult one, attended by portentous omens.

Zal's wife Rudabeh was ill, and getting weaker steadily as her confinement approached. In desperation her husband cast about for a cure – then remembered the Simurgh's feather, which the magical bird had told him to burn in time of need. He did so now, and almost at once the great creature hastened to answer his call.

The Simurgh listened carefully as Zal listed Rudabeh's symptoms, then sagely delivered its recommendations. A skilled doctor should be brought, it advised, to "pierce the frame of the young woman without her feeling any pain and draw the lion-child out of her" – in other words, to perform a Caesarean section under anaesthetic. The Simurgh itself provided an ointment to dress the wound as well as a feather to stroke over the scar, to help the healing process further. Then it benignly took its leave, soaring back towards its mountaintop home.

The suggestions worked, and a healthy boy was born. His parents named him Rustam, and even as a baby he was so robust that it took the milk of ten wetnurses to nourish him. He grew up to be something of a giant – as tall as a noble cypress, the poet claimed – and as handsome and intelligent as he was strong.

As for his courage, it quickly became legendary. Once, after he had gone to bed following an evening's drinking, he was awoken by sounds of commotion in the palace. Rushing outside, he learned that his father's great white elephant had run amok. Sobering up rapidly, he snatched up a battle-mace and hurried to confront the beast, knocking aside all who sought to stop him. The elephant charged him on sight, but he stood his ground. Roaring like a lion, he raised the mace and brought it down on the beast's head with such force that it dropped dead on the spot.

At the time Iran needed a champion, for the traditional rivalry with Turan to the northeast had been growing fiercer. When Manuchihr, Persia's King of Kings, died, the Turanian ruler Persheng had grown ambitious to seize the Persian throne for himself. He entrusted the task to his son

The Simurgh instructs Zal and Mehrab, king of Kabulestan, in the procedure of Caesarean section as Rudabeh is comforted by her mother. This illustration is from an 18th-century edition of the *Shahnameh* from Kashmir.

A Strong and Trusted Partner

Rakhsh was a steed fit for a hero, his partnership with Rustam foreordained by fate. Together they endured many dangerous adventures, and together they were to meet their untimely deaths.

A gold horse's head, dated to the Achaemenian period, c.6th–5th century BC.

When Rustam first embarked on a warrior's career, he set out to find a charger strong enough to bear his mighty weight and brave enough to face any danger. He had a simple test for the former; he would press the palm of his hand on a horse's back and see if its belly sagged to the ground. Even though he criss-crossed Iran looking for a suitable candidate, none of the beasts he examined would do.

It was in Turan that he finally found what he was looking for. He saw an unusually tall bay mare followed by a two-year-old colt of similar colour, flecked with red patches. He liked the look of the young horse, yet when he expressed an interest to the dealer, the man warned him not to get excited about another man's mount. When Rustam asked who the owner was, he was told that no one knew, but that it had always been known as Rustam's Rakhsh.

So the hero realized that he had found the steed fate had predestined for him. His choice was confirmed when he pressed on its back and found it firm as steel. And when the herdsman learned that his client was indeed Rustam, he would take no money, saying that the only payment he wanted was for man and steed together to bring justice to the world.

Afrasiab, a scheming prince who was fated to be Rustam's greatest enemy. But the Persians gave as good as they got, and Rustam distinguished himself in the fighting, outdoing all other warriors whether with mace, bow, sword or lance.

Then the Persian cause suffered an unforeseen setback. A series of short-lived monarchs succeeded Manuchihr as King of Kings, and at last the post fell to the rash and thoughtless Kay Kavus.

The trouble began when reports reached him of the wealth of the rarely visited province of Manzandaran, which lies in the mountains to the south of the Caspian Sea. At once he decided to seek an annual tribute from its king. When his envoys were rebuffed, he flew into a rage and impetuously determined to invade the land. In his haste he did not take the time to find out that Manzandaran's ruler was an evil spirit who benefited from the protection of the White Demon, a particularly terrifying *div*.

As a result of the *div*'s sorcery, he and his men soon found themselves bewitched. First they were attacked by a supernatural storm that literally blew away many of the finest warriors. Then a mist descended that robbed the remainder of their eyesight, leaving them to wander blindly on the plain outside the city.

Before this final disaster, Kay Kavus had sent a message to inform Zal of his plight. When Rustam heard that the King of Kings was in danger, he at once insisted on going in person to his aid. Worse still, however, he decided to take the shortest route to Manzandaran, even though his anxious father warned him that it led across trackless wastes known to be haunted by wild beasts and evil spirits.

The journey soon turned out to be an epic in miniature. In its course the young hero had to overcome seven mortal challenges, seen by some scholars as an echo of the twelve labours undertaken by the Greek hero, Herakles. First he was confronted by an angry lion that found him asleep in its lair. This menace was expertly dealt with by his horse Rakhsh (see box, page 77), which struck the beast down with its forelegs as its master slumbered; when the bewildered Rustam finally woke, the lion was already dead. Next the two had to cross a burning desert in which they almost died of thirst, only to stumble on an oasis just as they were at the point of collapse.

The Tricking of King Kavus

Like many kings before him, Kay Kavus fell victim through vanity to the wiles of a crafty div. The lesson that Kay Kavus learned, however, was not fatal – and can even be seen as comic.

One morning the demon came to the king in the form of a flattering courtier, telling him that, as he held sway over the entire Earth, the next logical step must be to extend his rule to the sky. The king fell into the trap, and took to brooding on the means by which he could mount the clouds to assert his sovereignty there also.

At last he came up with an idea. He had four eagles tethered to a throne to which he had himself strapped. Above the birds, legs of mutton were suspended on tall poles. As the eagles beat their wings to reach the sweet-smelling meat, they carried the throne up into the air, and soon the king found himself soaring through the sky.

But the birds were not inexhaustible, and when at last their strength began to flag, Kavus came down to earth with a bump. His experiment in aviation ended ignominiously in a forest somewhere in western China. It took a small army under the direction of Rustam to track him down and bring him back to Persia, crestfallen and – for the time being at least – repentant of his vanity and folly.

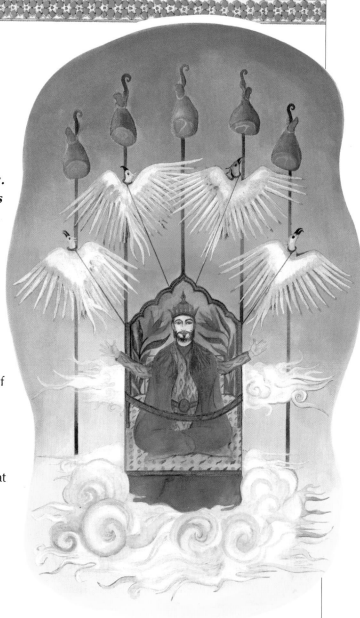

The third ordeal came when they took shelter in another cave – and made the same mistake as they had with the lion. Only after they had settled down to rest did they find out that it was the home of a deadly dragon with the power of making itself invisible at will. Again it was Rakhsh who first realized the danger while Rustam slept. But every time the horse tried to warn him, the dragon would disappear, convincing the warrior that his steed was simply suffering from bad nerves. Only on the monster's fourth appearance did he finally catch a glimpse of it. Then man and steed joined forces to give it short shrift.

The next trial was an encounter with a witch, who transformed herself into a ravishing young maiden and tempted Rustam with a delicious meal laid out invitingly by a pool in the desert. When the hero happened to mention the holy name of Ohrmazd, however, the odalisque turned into a hideous hag whom Rustam duly cut down with a single sword-stroke.

There followed a rather less heroic trial of strength with some frightened villagers whom Rustam easily cowed into submission, compelling their leader Aolad at swordpoint to lead him to the White Demon's lair. On the way they passed by Manzandaran, where they were joyfully welcomed by the still-blind Kay Kavus. The king urged the pair on to the final encounter, telling them that the White Demon itself had boasted that he and his men would never regain their sight until they were anointed with the blood of its own heart.

The demon, it turned out, lived in a cavern in the mountains high above the city. It was guarded by an army of lesser *div*, but Aolad revealed that they invariably slept for an hour or two in the midday heat, providing Rustam with a window of opportunity to reach his destination. Inside the cave he was set upon by guards, but he soon disposed of them with a flurry of sword blows.

The White Demon woke with a roar and hurled itself on the intruder. Rustam managed to slice a hand and a foot off his gigantic adversary with his first two sword-strokes, yet it still proved a formidable opponent. It clutched Rustam close

Rustam slays the White Demon of Manzandaran, in a detail from a 16th-century *Shahnameh*. This was the last of the seven dangerous tasks that Rustam was called upon to perform to prove his worthiness as Persia's greatest hero.

to its body, trying to squeeze the life out of him, but the hero managed to hold on until the demon had lost so much blood that its grip eventually began to weaken. Then with a final effort the hero managed to lift the monstrous being up into the air and hurl it to the floor, killing it instantly.

Victorious, Rustam returned to the city to find that the *div* who ruled it had fled. He brought with him the White Demon's heart, as instructed; a couple of drops of blood from it were enough to restore the sight of each soldier. Heaping praise on his rescuer for his skill and courage, Kay Kavus jubilantly led the force back home, having first established Rustam's guide Aolad on the throne of Manzandaran, which he ruled wisely as a tributary state of Persia for many years.

Sohrab and Rustam

The story of a long-lost son, found only to be cruelly snatched away by fate, is one of the best-known episodes of the *Shahnameh*. With its poisonous intrigues and epic finale, it also provides the bitterest tragedy of the entire Rustam saga.

Out hunting in hostile territory across the Turanian border one day, Rustam chanced upon a herd of wild asses. He gave thanks for his good fortune and, taking up his mighty bow, began killing many of the grazing animals. He then stoked up a great fire and prepared to enjoy the spoils of his successful expedition. After dining well on the roasted meat, he lay down to rest. But while he slept, a party of passing Turanian horsemen happened to catch sight of his steed Rakhsh. They marvelled at the horse and determined to steal it. This proved no easy task for as soon as they approached the wary animal it began kicking out with its legs. Rakhsh killed three of them as they struggled to lasso him. But at last they had him under control and made off to the nearby city of Samangan.

A 12th-century Persian jewel casket. Before he and his love Tahmineh were parted, Rustam gave her a jewelled amulet saying that were she to have a son she should give it to him as a gift from his father. This token of love was later to signal tragedy.

Rustam woke up to find Rakhsh gone, but by studying the hoofprints left at the scene of the theft he was able to piece together what had happened. Grimly, he set off on foot to follow the tracks of the men who had robbed him.

In Samangan he was greeted by the king, who, although a Turanian vassal, was eager to placate the angry champion whose home lay so close to his own borders. With honeyed words he assured his irate visitor that Rakhsh was far too famous to remain missing for long. Meanwhile, he offered him the hospitality of the palace while his men set off to hunt down the horse.

Mollified, Rustam accepted his offer. After dining well he retired to bed, only to be awoken in the middle of the night by an unexpected visitor. Roused from sleep, he found himself staring at an exquisitely beautiful girl whom he had never seen before in his life. His astonishment turned to amazement when she revealed that she was his host's daughter Tahmineh and that she had long been secretly in love with him on the strength of his reputation alone. Now that she had actually set eyes on him she could contain herself no longer and implored the startled Rustam to marry her at once.

Smitten by her beauty, the great hero wanted to find out how her father would react to the match, and was encouraged to learn that he welcomed the prospect of a family connection with so noble a warrior. So a priest was summoned and the two were wed there and then. Before the night was out they had consummated their union.

By the next morning Rakhsh had been found, and Rustam determined to head homewards. Before he left he told Tahmineh he would be back as soon as he could – but he knew that, because of the political divide that separated their two peoples, that might be a long time. With that in mind, he impulsively gave her the jewelled amulet he wore on his arm as a parting gift, telling her that if she should bear him a son, she should give the boy the talisman as a token of his father.

A New Turanian Hero

Nine months on a son was indeed born, and his mother named him Sohrab. He grew up to be his father's equal in strength, courage and virtue. For many years his mother kept the story of his birth a secret from him, but eventually his curiosity grew so great that she revealed that he was Rustam's son. From that time on the youth spent much of his time dreaming of his absent father, thinking of little except how to match the great warrior's achievements and win for himself a reputation that would make Rustam proud.

In pursuit of that goal he in time persuaded his grandfather to allow him to raise an army to make border raids into Iranian territory. Soon he began to make a name for himself as a warrior. Word reached Rustam of this new champion, and the thought that so brave a fighter might possibly be his long-lost son crossed his mind; but at once he dismissed it, persuading himself that no youth of Sohrab's tender years could possibly have achieved such feats of arms.

News of Sohrab's successes also got back to the Turanian king Afrasiab, who learned as well that the lad was Rustam's son – and that the two had never met. Slowly a plan began to take shape in his scheming mind.

Afrasiab's idea was that somehow the two warriors might be induced to fight one another. There was a tradition of single combat in the border wars, and both Sohrab and Rustam were the undisputed champions of their respective sides. But for his scheme to work it was essential that the two men should not recognize each other. So he sent warriors of his own to ride with the young man – and gave them strict orders not to identify Rustam to him if the two armies ever met face-to-face.

And so it eventually came to pass. In Iran's time of need, Rustam was summoned to lead the royal army in the field. When the two forces eventually met, Sohrab's first thought was whether his father might be in the ranks ranged against him. But the Iranian captive to whom he first put the question was so awed by his captor's strength that he chose to lie, fearing that otherwise Sohrab might challenge and defeat the great hero, with disastrous consequences for Persian morale.

So when the two warriors finally caught sight of each other across the battle-lines, each saw only an opponent of his own mettle rather than a possible kinsman. Rustam called out a challenge to the younger man, and Sohrab at once rose to it. Making their way onto neutral ground, the two looked one another over with a degree of respect unusual among enemies.

And yet when they at last addressed one another, it was with the ritual taunts of combatants preparing for a fight. Sohrab suggested that the older man, though a mighty figure no doubt, was now past the age for battles and should go his way in peace. Rustam responded by vaunting his past triumphs and saying that he had no desire to kill a mere youth.

Sohrab listened to all these boasts and began to admire his rival. The man's poise was so assured, his rhetoric so eloquent that Sohrab suddenly felt sure the unknown warrior must be his long-sought father. Unable to contain his excitement, he asked him outright if he was Rustam.

A 17th-century Persian helmet with nose guard. The elaborate designs reflect the rituals that surrounded combat in the early years of organized warfare. Since only the wealthiest of combatants could afford fine armour there was a tradition of single combat (see box, page 97). Much was made of show, however, and the exchange of boasts between Sohrab and Rustam before they fought was typical of such confrontations.

But now the older man's famed cunning, which had served him so well in past fights, caused him to make a tragic error. He feared that the young stranger wanted merely to boast of having met the great hero face-to-face on the battlefield and lived to tell the tale. Wishing to give no quarter to his enemy he lied outright, denying both the name and even any claim to nobility. Instead, his face darkened and his solicitous warnings gave way to angry jibes. Enough of words; he would reveal who he was in blows, not names.

The words of the Persian soldier at once broke the hopes of Sohrab's expectations. All thoughts now turned to conflict – and so father and son came together not in love and respect but in war. They fought with lances, then with swords, staves and bows. They struggled all day long, breaking off for the night only to face each other once more the following dawn. Again, Sohrab urged his adversary to put up his sword in the name of friendship. But Rustam's only answer was to call him grimly to battle.

The Warrior's Companion

Persian noblemen prized no treasure more highly than the steed that carried them into battle. For the horse was an indispensable tool of warfare and travel amid the vast Iranian plains – just as it had been since the time when nomadic Aryans rode into the region to alter the course of Persian history.

On the dry and dusty plains of ancient Persia, there was nothing more prized than a strong and reliable horse. Not only were horses essential battle equipment but also the principal means of transport, and as such they occupy a special place throughout the *Shahnameh*.

The tragedy of Sohrab and Rustam begins with the theft of Rakhsh, and Sohrab's first concern when he embarks on a military career is to find a mount worthy of the triumphs he has dreamed for himself.

In this respect the stories reflected historical reality, for the Aryans who conquered Persia and India in the second millennium BC relied on horse-drawn chariots for much of their military superiority. Horses also occupied a special place in their religion. In early times, in a ritual that may have come from India, where animals were offered to the gods, the most sacred gift of all was the horse. A prized stallion was allowed to roam freely for a year before being ritually slaughtered.

The figure of a horse is immortalized on this thin sheet of pure gold, found by the Oxus River and dating to the 5th–4th century BC.

That day the two wrestled, and after a time Sohrab got the upper hand. Forcing the older man to the ground, he drew a dagger to deliver the mortal blow. But wily Rustam called out to him to hold back, telling him that by Persian custom a wrestler must be felled twice before he could honourably be killed. So Sohrab stayed his hand and even granted his opponent a respite, giving the old tiger time to refresh himself and renew his energy for the struggle.

In that brief pause Rustam prayed to God, and perhaps his prayers were answered, for the old warrior came back stronger than ever. Now even Sohrab could not withstand his fierce onslaught. Using all his strength and cunning, Rustam forced his opponent to the ground. Then, unmoved by the qualms that had gripped his son, he drew his own dagger and plunged it into the younger man's breast.

Sohrab knew at once that he was done for. To stop his victorious foe from triumphing, he warned him not to crow over his victory. His death, he said, would be avenged – for even if he became a fish in water, or like darkness in the night or a star in the sky, his killer would be tracked down by his own father, Persia's greatest hero, Rustam.

When the old warrior heard that terrible word, the world suddenly grew dark about him. Desperately, he asked for proof of what the young man said. He found himself looking at the amulet he had given so many years before to Tahmineh.

Forced to accept the truth, he sank to his knees, seeking to staunch the flow of blood from his son's wound with his fingers. Then he cradled the boy in his lap and listened as he spoke of the dreams he had hoped to realize and the ambitions he would never fulfil. He stayed there unmoving throughout the long hours of the day, until the first stars were showing in the cold night sky.

In time emissaries were sent to fetch him, but at first he did not hear them. Only when one spoke hopefully of a healing balm that might yet save his son did he finally rouse himself, calling out for Rakhsh, who had been waiting patiently nearby on the darkening plain, dimly aware of his

A heartbroken Rustam watches the dying Sohrab reveal the amulet he had given Tahmineh, from a 17th-century illustrated edition of the *Shahnameh*, from Isfahan. Before they began fighting, Sohrab had asked Rustam to reveal his identity – but, tragically, the Persian hero had lied.

master's sorrow. But there was to be no happy ending. The old warrior had scarcely raised himself into the saddle when he heard a cry from one of the aides who had stayed by the young man's side. Numbly Rustam dismounted, hardly needing confirmation of what he instinctively knew. Sohrab, his only son, had finally passed away.

83

An Ill-Starred Prince

Brave, handsome and nobly born, Siyavush seemingly had every advantage that fate could bestow. And with none other than the noble Rustam to teach him the arts of war and leisure, he seemed surely set for greatness. His destiny, however, was tragic.

One day the Persian generals Tus and Gudarz, along with Gudarz's son Giv, were hunting near the Turanian border when they came across an unexpected sight. They found a beautiful maiden wandering alone in the depths of a forest. When they asked her what she was doing there, she replied that she had run away from her father, who had beaten her. On the way she had been attacked by thieves who had stolen her horse and all the valuables she had brought with her, for she was a noblewoman who could trace her descent to both the Iranian and Turanian royal lines.

The hunters were captivated by her beauty, and Tus and Giv were soon quarrelling over who had the first claim upon her. To stop them fighting, one of the other huntsmen suggested taking the girl back to King Kavus. When they did so, the monarch was equally smitten and was delighted when – given a free choice of partners – the girl selected him, becoming one of the many wives in the royal harem.

In due course she bore Kay Kavus a son, whom the couple named Siyavush. They decided to send him to Rustam for his education, knowing no one better fitted to train a youth in the noble arts. From the older man Siyavush learned horsemanship, archery and falconry and the skills of hunting with a cheetah. He also studied oratory and warfare, and was shown how to behave at banquets and ceremonies.

Siyavush returned to the palace as an accomplished courtier. But his very virtues almost caused his downfall, for they attracted

the attention of the king's principal wife, Sudabeh, who before long was hopelessly in love with him. But when she confessed her affection the prince rejected her. She was distraught and at once revenged herself in a particularly malignant way: she falsely accused him before Kay Kavus of trying to violate her – a charge the prince angrily denied.

Faced by two directly conflicting stories from his favourite wife and son, the king did not know whom to believe. Eventually he decided that there was only one way to determine the truth of the claims, and that was to have recourse to an ancient ritual used to root out falsehood. Either Sudabeh or Siyavush must undergo ordeal by fire.

The queen refused outright, but Siyavush, sure of his innocence, agreed at once. So the king had two huge mounds of brushwood prepared and set alight. Dressed in white and with a golden crown on his head, the young prince approached the flames mounted on a black charger. Whispering a prayer, he spurred his mount into the hottest part of the blaze.

Deep silence fell on the assembled onlookers. Then a cry arose from the far side of the bonfire: "The prince is safe!" As the proud white figure emerged from the smoke, the shout echoed from countless mouths. Siyavush had survived the trial unscathed.

Now Kay Kavus no longer had any doubt of his son's innocence. At first he planned to have Sudabeh executed for her perfidy, but Siyavush generously pleaded for her life, and she was allowed to remain at court, sequestered in the women's quarters.

The Menace of Afrasiab

Meanwhile news reached the court that Persia's old enemy, Afrasiab of Turan, was once more threatening the nation's borders. The king turned to Siyavush, who agreed to command the Iranian army, taking Rustam with him as his chief lieutenant.

The appointment turned out to be well omened, for not long afterwards Afrasiab was tormented with a fearful nightmare. In it he found himself gazing across a desert writhing

The arts of hunting and war both employed the skills of archery and horsemanship, as shown on this 15th-century book cover. Mastery of these disciplines, however, failed to help Siyavush, who was confounded by fate alone.

85

A Legendary Line of Kings

In its entirety, the Shahnameh tells the story of many reigns, thirty-five of which can be equated with real-life monarchs whose deeds are well recorded in historical manuscripts.

Firdowsi's starting-point for his epic seems to have been a list of historical kings, but within it more than one tradition was evidently represented. The legendary kings of the earlier part of the work are mostly those known otherwise from the *Avesta* and have little if anything to do with the Achaemenian rulers who actually ruled Persia in its first time of glory. Intermingled with their story is the legendary history of the rulers of Sistan, of whom Sam, Zal and Rustam were the most famous.

Scholars now think that these stories were based on the deeds of the Saka dynasty that ruled an area of eastern Iran in the Parthian period around the start of the Christian era – an epoch of which Firdowsi claimed to know little. The only section of his work that relates directly to the known historical record is the last part, which presents a comparatively factual record of the reigns of the Sasanian kings who ruled Iran from AD224 to the end of the Arab conquest in 651.

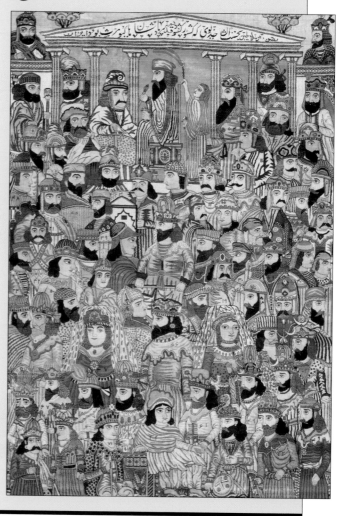

A 19th-century Kirman carpet depicts the massed ranks of Persian kings from Kiyumars to the Sasanians. Behind them stands a classical temple portico.

with serpents. As he watched, a dust-storm arose on the horizon, hurrying ever closer. It was almost upon him before he realized that it was stirred up by enemy horsemen, each bearing a lance with a skull at the tip. Unable to flee, the Turanian ruler saw the mounted warriors bear him away as a prisoner to Kay Kavus's court, where a handsome youth – Siyavush, as he later realized – stepped forward to cleave him in two with a mighty scimitar. As the blade flashed through the air, the terrified Afrasiab woke up screaming.

Sages were quickly summoned who confirmed that the dream presaged a terrible defeat at the hand of the Persians. Their advice was enough to persuade the Turanian leader to sue for peace. Negotiations were begun in which he agreed to restore all the land he had occupied. As proof of his good intentions, he sent rich gifts to Siyavush and willingly handed over a hundred of his finest warriors as hostages.

Siyavush was delighted with his triumph, and expected his father to be equally pleased. But when Rustam bore news of the truce back to the Persian court, Kay Kavus could barely restrain his anger. He wanted nothing less than Afrasiab's destruction; and with that in mind he commanded that the gifts should all be burned and the hostages sent to him be beheaded at once.

Rustam was aghast, for Siyavush had personally guaranteed the warriors' safety. He told Kay Kavus his feelings in no uncertain terms, and for his pains he was exiled from the court. Meanwhile a message was sent summoning the prince back in disgrace. Tus was appointed commander of the army in his stead.

When Siyavush learned of this unexpected turn of events, he was plunged into despair. Thinking himself at the top of fortune's wheel, he suddenly found himself cast down into the depths. His own dismissal was bad enough, but the thought that the Turanian hostages might be killed in spite of his pledge troubled him even more. In his agony of mind, he came to a desperate decision: he would go over to the Turanians, casting himself on the mercy of the enemy.

In fact no news could have better pleased Afrasiab, who ordered the unexpected refugee to be given a hero's welcome. The Turanian ruler's joy was all the greater when he learned that the turmoil caused by Siyavush's defection and the departure of Rustam had persuaded the ever-volatile Kay Kavus to change his mind once more and order a cessation of hostilities.

A Turanian Courtier

Time passed, and Siyavush built a new life for himself at the Turanian court. At first Afrasiab favoured him, giving him his own daughter Ferangis as a wife and appointing him governor of the province of Khotan. Once more it seemed that fate was smiling on him despite his sudden change of allegiance.

But he had enemies in his new home, and it was not long before they began plotting against him. Foremost among the conspirators was Afrasiab's brother Garsivaz, who saw his own position at court threatened by the honours heaped on the new favourite. So he set out to undermine Siyavush's place in the ruler's esteem, insinuating that the prince was disloyal and was secretly plotting to defect once more, taking Khotan over to the Persian camp.

At first Afrasiab refused to believe him. Eventually, though, doubts entered his mind, and he summoned Siyavush to court to answer them. Now Garsivaz played a double-game, representing to the prince that the ruler's mind had been poisoned against him and that his life would be in danger if he obeyed the order. Siyavush hesitated, and the delay was enough to persuade Afrasiab of the truth of the charges of disloyalty that had been levelled against him.

Fate, it seemed, had turned against Siyavush once more, again through no fault of his own. This time the reversal of fortune was to be final. Egged on by his wife, he decided to flee to Persia. Word of his flight spread rapidly and he was quickly overtaken by pursuing troops. He was captured easily, then dragged back as a prisoner to his own palace. That very night he was savagely done to death by a henchman of Garsivaz, who cut off his head as he lay bound and unarmed and collected his blood in a bowl.

And so a life that had begun with every show of promise ended tragically in treachery and bloodshed. Seeking only to do what was honourable, Siyavush had become destiny's plaything; and in the end he found himself forsaken, cast aside by fate like a discarded toy.

The humiliation of Siyavush continued beyond his death when his savage vanquisher, a henchman of Garsivaz, drained his blood and collected it in a bowl. This silver dish, engraved with a gold horse and rider, dates from the 8th century.

The Battle with Akvan

Not all of Rustam's battles were with human adversaries. He also fought *div*, and none was more fearsome than the dreaded Akvan. Capable of assuming animal form and possessed of the powers of invisibility, this demon proved one of Rustam's most troublesome foes.

One day a herdsman came before the King of Kings complaining that his horses were being plagued by a big and powerful ass. When the king learned that the beasts were kept near a spring that had long been known as the home of a particularly ferocious *div* named Akvan, he concluded that the strange aggressor could only be this fearsome demon in animal form.

The king looked to Rustam as the only man fit for the challenge. The hero accepted and immediately set off for the spring. For three days he waited for a sight of the ass, and had almost given up hope when suddenly he saw it galloping across the plain. It was indeed a monstrous creature, and his first thought was to lasso it and capture it alive to show to the king. But the moment he threw the rope the beast simply vanished from sight, reappearing moments later some distance away.

This unnatural behaviour was quite enough to convince Rustam that he was indeed dealing with Akvan, and he decided at once that extreme measures were needed. Abandoning all thoughts of taking the beast alive, he fitted an arrow to his bow instead. But just as he was about to loose it, the ass once more disappeared from view, materializing seconds later a little farther off. This time the hero drew his sword and charged, but it fled before him, vanishing without trace whenever he threatened to get close.

For a day and a night Rustam pursued the elusive creature until he was ready to drop with fatigue. Spotting a spring of fresh water, he dismounted and lay down to rest. Almost at once he fell asleep.

Seeing his enemy at a disadvantage, Akvan took the chance to go on the attack. Transforming himself into a whirlwind, he rushed up to Rustam and spun in a circle round him, cutting the earth

The sleeping Rustam is carried off by the demon Akvan before being thrown into the sea, from a 16th-century illustration of the *Shahnameh*.

Mountains tower over a lake near the Caspian Sea in northern Iran. Rustam knew his only chance of survival was to be dropped into the water, from where he could swim to safety.

from under the sleeping warrior. Then he sucked him high up into the air. When Rustam awoke it was to find himself up among the clouds, looking down on the land far below.

The demon, chuckling evilly at his discomfort, offered him a choice: he could be dropped on the mountains, where the impact would shatter his bones, or in the ocean to drown. Rustam thought quickly. He knew that the sea was his best option, as it offered at least a slim chance of survival, but he was also aware that *div* in their perversity usually did the opposite of what their victims asked. So he said he preferred to die on the mountainside, where at least his remains could be gathered, ensuring him an honourable burial.

As he had suspected, Akvan at once headed seawards, and soon the hero found himself plunging from a great height down into the waves. He sank to the ocean bottom, but fought his way back to the surface, his lungs almost bursting for lack of air. Then he struck out for land, holding his sword in his hand as he swam to fight off the sharks that constantly circled around him.

Akvan had dropped him far from shore, but drawing on his great reserves of strength, he eventually flopped onto a sandy beach, half-dead with exhaustion but with his weapons still about him. When he had rested, he made his way back to the spring where he had left Rakhsh – but his loyal steed was gone. He eventually found him attached to a group of horses belonging to Afrasiab, the great enemy of Persia, and took pleasure in reclaiming not just his own mount but also in driving off the entire herd while their Turanian guards chased impotently after them.

After shaking off his pursuers, Rustam came back once more to Akvan's spring where he still had unfinished business to settle. The *div* was so startled to see a man he had thought safely dead standing large as life before him that for a brief, fatal instant he forgot to make himself invisible. Rustam had just the time he needed to cast his lasso over the demon's head, preventing the *div* from getting away. Then, as it struggled in the meshes, he brought down his battle-axe on the monster's head. Cutting off what was left of the skull with his dagger, he took the trophy back to the royal court, and all the knights of Persia marvelled at the might of a warrior for whom even the fiercest *div* were no match.

89

The Wars Between Iran and Turan

The death of Siyavush proved the catalyst for a series of wars between Iran and Turan in which each side, like Homer's Greeks and Trojans, looked to individual heroes to sway the course of the struggle their way.

Although he defected to the Turanians, Siyavush became by his death the great martyr of Persian legend. His murder came to be regarded as the ultimate example of the duplicity of Turan, and all Persia's heroes vowed to avenge it.

The first to act, as usual, was Rustam. Blaming Kay Kavus's wife Sudabeh for starting the trouble, he rushed into the women's quarters of the palace in a blind fury and cut her down with his sword.

Then he set off with an army for Turan, defeated the Turanian leader Afrasiab in single combat, put his troops to flight and ravaged the country, spreading devastation in his wake.

Meanwhile, Siyavush's son Kay Khusrow was growing up in the province of Khotan where he had been taken for his own protection. Reared by shepherds, he grew to adolescence, strong, handsome and in every respect fit to be a king.

Echoes of History and Myth

Legends concerning the childhood of the real-life monarch Cyrus the Great suggest that this great historical king might have served as a model for the fictional Kay Khusrow who, in the **Shahnameh**, *emerges as one of the mightiest of Persia's early rulers.*

Cyrus, who lived in the sixth century BC, was one of the greatest rulers of antiquity. The founder of the Achaemenian dynasty and creator of the first Persian empire, he rose to power by defeating Astyages, the king of the Medes, in single combat. After his death, stories about his birth and upbringing reached the ears of the historian Herodotus, who recorded them for posterity.

As the Greek told the story, Astyages was Cyrus's grandfather. In a dream he received a warning that his daughter, Mandaneh, would bear a son who would one day usurp his throne. Accordingly, he took her baby from her as soon as it was born, and gave it to a nobleman named Harpagus with strict orders to kill it. Harpagus, however, passed the boy to a herdsman in the country who brought him up as his own child in the safety of the hills.

When Astyages found out that Harpagus had disobeyed him, he took a horrible revenge. He had the nobleman's own son secretly killed, then served up to the unsuspecting father at a court dinner. Harpagus only learned the true nature of the meal at its end, when the cover was removed from the final dish to reveal his son's head. But Astyages was not to go unpunished – for in the meantime, while these horrors were being perpetrated at court, Cyrus was growing up to be a regal youth, and in due course he left his flocks to become the king that destiny had ordained for him.

The story has similarities with that of Kay Khusrow, as it is told in the *Shahnameh*. According to the epic, Kay Khusrow was also taken away from court when he was a child and brought up by a herdsman, and his future greatness was similarly foretold in a dream, in his case to his father Siyavush before his murder. These links, and the likeness of the Persian forms of the names, may suggest that elements of the Cyrus story influenced the legends of Khusrow, even though the two monarchs' later careers had little in common.

Then bad news came. Worried by a prophecy that Siyavush's son would cause his own downfall, Afrasiab told Piran, the boy's protector, that his ward must be killed. Searching desperately for a way to save Kay Khusrow, Piran sought to calm the ruler's fears by insisting that the boy was an idiot. The young prince was summoned to the palace and, having practised giving senseless answers to any question put to him, demonstrated the truth of the claim. The monarch was happy to let him go back safely to his sheep.

It was a mistake, for at roughly the same time the ageing Kay Kavus was looking for a successor to act as his regent. Discounting his son Fariburz, who was brave but ill-equipped to be king, the monarch's thoughts turned instead to his grandson Kay Khusrow, far away in Turan.

The problem was that no one in Persia knew exactly where Kay Khusrow was. A warrior named Giv was sent to find him, and he eventually tracked him down in Khotan. He easily persuaded the young man and his mother to travel with him back to Iran, but word of their flight soon reached Afrasiab and the journey turned into a desperate chase. The trio finally arrived at the Oxus River, which separated the two empires. With Afrasiab himself at their heels, they rode their horses through the flooded stream, a feat considered impossible until that time.

Kay Khusrow was given a hero's welcome and Kay Kavus announced his intention of standing down from the throne and passing it to the young warrior. The only dissenter was Tus, an ally of Fariburz. Briefly, the threat of civil war loomed.

The tomb of Cyrus stands tall on the flat plain around Pasargadae, the site of his capital in the south of Iran. The city was begun around 546BC and prompted Darius to build his magnificent palace at Persepolis nearby. Cyrus's cenotaph, however, remained for many generations of Persian kings the abiding symbol of their country's greatness.

To break the deadlock, Kay Kavus proposed to test the mettle of the two rival claimants. He challenged them to capture a stronghold in the Iranian borderlands that was said to be guarded by demons. Fariburz made the first attempt, but found the task impossible; the fortress hovered in the air, had neither gate nor window, and was surrounded by a ring of flames. Yet Kay Khusrow found a simple way to penetrate its defences, by writing the name of God on a pennant and raising it on the tip of his lance. At the mere sight of the holy banner, the flames died down and the fortress sank to earth, revealing a perfectly normal gateway that had been hidden by enchantment. Kay Khusrow entered and drove out the demons, putting the question of his fitness to rule beyond dispute.

His reign forms the narrative core of the *Shahnameh*, for in it the struggle between Iran and Turan is at its height. The ebb and flow of the various campaigns recall the fighting in Homer's *Iliad*, not least in the decisive role played by individual heroes in shaping the fortunes of battle.

Kay Khusrow's First Campaigns

The fighting began at the very start of the reign, for virtually Kay Khusrow's first act was to launch an invasion of Turan to avenge his father Siyavush.

That initial campaign went badly for the Persians. Tus disobeyed orders to respect the integrity of the border state of Kalat, ruled by Kay Khusrow's own half-brother Farud. In the ensuing strife, Farud himself was needlessly killed, along with many Persian warriors.

Worse was to follow. Tus and Giv allowed discipline to slip in the ranks to such an extent that the Turanians were able to rout the Persians in a surprise attack, launched at night when many of the Persians were drunkenly celebrating their supposed invincibility.

As a result, Tus was immediately recalled in disgrace and placed under house arrest. Fariburz, the defeated contender for the throne, was given command of the army in his place. He took one look at his demoralized troops and decided he needed time to reorganize. He asked the enemy for a one-month truce, and the honourable Piran – still entrusted by Afrasiab with control of the Turanian army despite his role in saving Kay Khusrow's life – agreed to grant it. Despite his unwonted leniency, the Iranians were worsted again when the truce came to an end, and despondently retreated back to Persia. The Turanians had won a famous victory.

Even so, the Persians were only down and not out. They had an unused weapon in Rustam, who led the troops in a renewed assault on Afrasiab's forces that quickly turned into a bloody stalemate. To break it, the Turanians used sorcery, sending a renowned magic-maker called Baru up a nearby mountainside to summon a tempest. Blinded by darkness, hail and snow, the Persians were hard put to survive until, in answer to their prayers, a mysterious stranger appeared to lead one of their heroes to Baru. The warrior cut off the wonder-worker's arms, reducing him to impotence since he could no longer carry out his invocations.

Yet the Persians' problems were still far from over. The Turanians drove them back to the mountains, where they took refuge in a fortress to recoup their strength. Afrasiab took advantage of the lull to summon fresh champions of his own: a fearsome trio from the Chinese and Indian borderlands named Shinkul of Sugsar, Kamus of Kushan and the Khaghan of Chin.

In the renewed fighting that followed, Rustam came into his own. Single-handedly he overcame all three of the warlords summoned against him. The Turanian forces were eventually driven from the field. For a time the Persians were again able to ravage Turan unchecked, doing particular damage to Khotan to avenge Siyavush's death. In time, however, Afrasiab managed to equip a new army, led by a fresh champion named Puladvand whom he hoped would at last prove more than a match even for Rustam.

Puladvand indeed proved a formidable opponent. When the two armies met, he not only trussed up Tus and Giv with his lasso but even succeeded in cutting Persia's famous fighting banner, the Kaviani standard, in two. This indignity was more than Rustam could bear, however, and in a climactic showdown the two heroes met face-to-face on the open plain.

They agreed to test their strength in a wrestling match. When Rustam got the upper hand, however, Afrasiab treacherously urged Puladvand to kill him with his dagger, against all the conventions of unarmed combat. This act of

A Persian warrior attacks Baru, in an illustrated *Shahnameh*, c.1440. Baru had summoned storms to confound the Persian armies and ensure victory for Turan.

treachery so incensed Rustam that he dashed his rival to the ground, where he lay as though dead. Even though he turned out to be merely winded, his defeat was the last straw for Afrasiab, who abandoned the field and went into hiding. Rustam was able to return in triumph to Iran, where Kay Khusrow greeted him joyfully in the knowledge that the nation's honour had been fully restored.

93

Kay Khusrow's Final Victory

Rustam's triumph did not mark the end of the wars with Turan. The conflict between Kay Khusrow and Afrasiab was so bitter that it could only be resolved by death. But the terrible climax was ushered in not by revenge, but through love.

Fighting between the two nations broke out again in an unexpected way. When a herd of wild boar began ravaging a district near the Turanian border, Giv's son Bizhan offered to get rid of the beasts. While doing so he found himself in Turan, and there chanced to meet Afrasiab's youngest daughter, Manizheh, who was staying in the region.

The two at once fell in love. In fact the princess was so besotted with the Persian that, when they had to part, she drugged his drink and smuggled him back to her father's palace. There they lived together in secret – until they were discovered by Afrasiab's guards.

When Bizhan was dragged before him, the furious Turanian king sentenced him to be thrown in chains into a deep pit, its entrance blocked up by a huge boulder. He also disowned his daughter, who followed her lover to his prison and managed to keep him alive by passing bread and water to him through a crack in the rock.

Word of his predicament soon reached the Persian court and Rustam at once determined to rescue him. Disguised as merchants, he and seven companions travelled through Turan until they found out where he was. Rustam at once used his gigantic strength to raise the boulder blocking the pit, and they pulled the emaciated prisoner to safety.

Before taking Bizhan and Manizheh back to Iran, Rustam could not resist raiding Afrasiab's palace. Entering the building unnoticed, he and his companions rushed into the throne room with swords drawn, sending the Turanian ruler fleeing for his life. They then looted his treasures and set off back to Persia before he could rally his troops to pursue them.

The insult was too much for proud Afrasiab to bear and his thoughts turned once more to war. But all the ruler's attempts to revenge earlier defeats were to prove unsuccessful. Although he called up fresh champions to take on Rustam, and even concocted a plot to poison him along with the other Persian leaders, all his efforts came to nothing. His army was once more routed.

Seizing the initiative, Kay Khusrow then sent an expedition of his own against Turan under the command of Giv's father Gudarz. The ensuing war raged unabated for two long years without either side gaining a decisive advantage. Then the Turanians suffered a mortal blow. Afrasiab's finest general, the chivalrous Piran, was slain.

Manizheh drugged Bizhan's drink through love while Afrasiab planned to poison Rustam's in hate. A *rhyton*, or ritual drinking cup, c.5th century BC.

The Corrupting Power of Kings

Kay Khusrow is the nearest thing to an ideal monarch in the Shahnameh. *Celebrated for his success in war, he was also noted for his wisdom – but he was always wary of the corrupting influence of power.*

The *Shahnameh* is all about kings, and one of its intriguing features is the attitude its author Firdowsi takes to their powers. He never questions the need for monarchical rule, seeing it as the only alternative to anarchy. Yet he is far from uncritical of individual rulers, portraying some – notably Kay Kavus – as not fit for the high responsibilities placed upon them.

His sense of royal accountability comes over strongly in his treatment of Kay Khusrow, whom he portrays as almost without flaws. Even so, this paragon shows in a revealing monologue shortly before his abdication an awareness of the dangers of absolute power. "I shall turn to crookedness and unwisdom and shall pass away into darkness," he muses, contemplating what might happen if he were to remain on the throne. "In this world, all that will remain of me will be ill repute; and an evil end will await me when I come before God."

A Sasanian silver-gilt dish depicting a king on his throne supported by ibexes and winged horses.

Kay Khusrow himself then led the final assault. Having defeated and killed Afrasiab's own son in single combat, he went on to drive the Turanian ruler and his men from the field.

The Persians pursued Afrasiab across country while his few remaining followers slowly fell away. Eventually he was quite alone. He took refuge in a cave in the mountains, hoping to evade detection. But a local hermit who had suffered wrong at his hands discovered him and handed him over to the enemy. He was led before Kay Khusrow, who turned down his appeal for mercy. Then the Persian monarch personally beheaded him and his brother Garsivaz, collecting their blood in a bowl just as the Turanians had done so many years before when Siyavush was killed.

Soon afterwards Kay Kavus died, leaving Kay Khusrow sole ruler of Iran. He reigned for sixty years, and then a time came when he too lost his appetite for life. He had accomplished everything he had set out to achieve and now the hour had arrived to turn his mind to God. Accordingly, he abdicated in favour of Lohrasp, another grandson of Kay Kavus. Then, taking leave of the warriors who had served him so faithfully, he left the palace and made his way towards the mountains. Some of his closest followers went with him, but eventually he waved them back, telling them that a snow-storm was coming that they would not survive. Watching from a distance, they saw him disappear into it high up on the mountainside. It was the last anyone ever saw of the king.

95

Valorous Isfandiyar

After Rustam, Isfandiyar was the mightiest hero ancient Persia ever knew for, according to legend, he had been made invulnerable by Zoroaster himself. This claim, however, was tested when a cruel twist of fate brought the two warriors face-to-face in mortal combat.

After Kay Khusrow's disappearance, the Persian throne passed to Lohrasp, who eventually abdicated to devote himself to religion. He handed over the crown to his son Gushtasp, a bold warrior with an overweening lust for power. His avidity would one day bring him into conflict with his own son Isfandiyar, who shared his ambitious nature but outmatched him in strength and ability.

As Firdowsi tells the story, it was in Gushtasp's reign that Zoroaster brought fire-worship to Persia. He zealously propagated the faith, and the king was an early convert.

War, however, was his primary concern, for a fresh leader had arisen in Turan who was eager to renew the struggle with the Persians. His name was Arjasp, and he demanded tribute from the Iranian ruler. When Gushtasp refused, war broke out once more between the two powers.

It was in the ensuing fighting that Isfandiyar established his reputation. The commander of the Persian forces was Gushtasp's brother Zarir, but he was killed early on in the conflict. The young Isfandiyar then took command in the dead general's place, leading the Persians to a famous victory. To reward him, Gushtasp had him crowned, formally recognizing him as his successor when he died – or when he decided, as Lohrasp had before him, to step down from power.

Buoyed up by ambition, Isfandiyar now embarked on a career of conquest, carrying Persia's new Zoroastrian faith eastwards into Hindustan and westwards into Arabia and the Mediterranean lands. For a time he seemed unstoppable, until his very successes brought him down. For they aroused the envy of Gushtasp, who feared his own fame was being eclipsed by the progress of his victorious son.

So when a warrior named Gurzam came to him with false claims that the prince wanted to depose him, Gushtasp was easily persuaded. He summoned Isfandiyar back to Balkh and had him seized by palace guards. Unexpectedly, the world conqueror found himself imprisoned in chains.

Militarily, the results of this regal coup were disastrous. With no leader to guide it the demoralized Persian army disbanded – and instead of acting swiftly and taking the situation in hand, the rash Gushtasp chose this time to travel to Sistan to stay with Rustam.

So when Arjasp sent an army to attack Balkh, he found the Persian capital virtually undefended. In desperation, the inhabitants persuaded Lohrasp to emerge from seclusion and lead a force to save the city. But the aged sovereign's troops were no match for the invaders, and in the ensuing battle he himself was killed and the city was taken.

Appalled, Gushtasp looked to Rustam for help, only to be turned down; happy to stay at home, the hero used his age and failing health as excuses for not joining the fray. So the King of Kings himself had to take the field in an attempt to relieve Balkh, only to see his forces driven back by the Turanians.

In this time of trial, Gushtasp turned to his astrologers for help, and was told that there was only one man who could save Iran: the imprisoned Isfandiyar. It was time for Gushtasp to admit past mistakes, so he freed his son and, with many humble apologies, begged his forgiveness.

The Age of Single Combat

Face-to-face confrontations between kings' champions, warriors like Rustam, Sohrab or Isfandiyar, could sway the outcome of entire battles in the heroic age before tactical battle-plans.

Single combat was a distinctive feature of late Bronze Age warfare not just in Persia but also throughout much of the Mediterranean world. It plays a prominent role in Homer's *Iliad* as well as in such Biblical confrontations as the clash between David and Goliath and forms a central feature of the *Shahnameh*. One reason for its prevalence was the expensive nature of metal at the time, which meant that a small, aristocratic elite of wealthy warriors had exclusive access to the best weaponry. Another lay in unsophisticated battlefield tactics that favoured individual prowess over disciplined teamwork. Once armies became organized into phalanxes and legions and the spread of iron had democratized the military arsenal, the hero who could turn the fortunes of a battle by individual feats of arms had largely had his day. Such actions, however, lived on as the very stuff of epic poetry throughout the world.

Elaborately decorated Persian body armour, with breastplates and back panels, c.1737.

Isfandiyar agreed to take command of the army again, and once more he was able to carry the day. Balkh was relieved and Arjasp's forces were sent fleeing back to Turan. But after the triumph one piece of unfinished business remained: two of the prince's sisters were still in Turanian hands, and word had it that they were held captive in Arjasp's stronghold, the Brazen Fortress.

Isfandiyar decided to rescue them himself. Gushtasp provided him with a force of picked men, and also with the services of a Turanian captive who offered to guide the Persians in return for his freedom. When the prince asked him the way to the Brazen Fortress, he replied that there were three routes: an easy one that took three months,

a less pleasant one needing eight weeks, and one that could be covered in seven days, though on every day some monster or terrible challenge would have to be overcome. Isfandiyar instantly opted for the short, perilous path.

And so, like Rustam before him (see page 78), the younger man undertook seven trials. On the first stage of the journey, he was called on to kill two ravening wolves, on the second a lion and lioness. Next he used an ingenious contraption to kill a dragon (see box below), while on the fourth day he dispatched a sorceress and her attendant demon. Then he encountered the Simurgh (see page 108), which – unlike Zal – he treated as an enemy and killed. Subsequent events were to

Isfandiyar and the Dragon

Isfandiyar's most ingenious exploit was an inventive feat of dragon-slaying.

One of the trials confronting Isfandiyar on his way to the Brazen Fortress was a vast and venomous dragon that swallowed travellers whole. To confront this monster, the prince had a carriage constructed whose roof and sides were stuck with lances and sword-blades like a pin-cushion. He then harnessed it to a pair of horses to approach the creature's lair. As soon as he heard its threatening roar, he got inside the vehicle and closed the door tightly.

Furious at the intrusion, the dragon swallowed vehicle and horses in one gulp. But the sharp points stuck in its throat, lacerating it horribly. Eventually it was forced to disgorge the lethal mouthful in a flood of blood. In a trice the prince leaped from the carriage and dealt the monster a death-blow with his sword. Even so, the poison that swept over him from the wound sent him reeling, and it was some time before he could celebrate his victory.

Isfandiyar uses his ingenious carriage to kill the dragon, in a detail from a 15th-century illustrated Shahnameh.

show that he might have done better to court its friendship. The last two obstacles were a blinding snowstorm that threatened to freeze his men to death, and a desert stretch of burning sands, which he managed to negotiate successfully.

Isfandiyar finally came to the Brazen Fortress, which at first sight seemed impregnable. Eventually he decided that the only possible way in was through deception. So he dressed himself up as a merchant and disguised his baggage camels as a traders' caravan complete with baskets of rich wares – except that inside the paniers of all but the first few beasts he had put not fine cloths and jewellery but armed warriors.

Bored inside his fortress, Arjasp was happy to receive a luxury-goods vendor – especially when the stranger offered to treat him and his courtiers to a banquet. A splendid meal was duly served. Then, when the Turanian monarch and his warriors were well and truly in their cups, Isfandiyar brought an end to the charade by revealing who he was and loosing his warriors on the revellers. The result was a massacre in which both Arjasp himself and his son were savagely killed.

Isfandiyar returned in triumph to Balkh, hoping that at last Gushtasp would abdicate in his favour. But his ambitions only reawakened the old monarch's fears. Consulting his seers once more, he received some startling information: one day Isfandiyar would be killed by Rustam.

Brooding on the prediction, Gushtasp gradually formed a plan. He had been eager anyway to punish Rustam for failing to come to his aid after Balkh was taken. Now he saw a way of killing two birds with one stone. He gave Isfandiyar orders to bring Rustam to him in chains; if he did so, Gushtasp promised, he would at last step down from the throne.

At first Isfandiyar demurred at the task of humiliating Iran's greatest hero, but ambition spurred him on. So he travelled to Sistan and demanded Rustam's submission. Although the older man had no desire for a fight, there was no way he would consent to be bound. A battle of the champions became inevitable.

And so Rustam and Isfandiyar met in single combat, as Gushtasp had known they would. Rustam was by now growing old, and victory would almost certainly have gone to his younger opponent but for a secret weapon on which he and his father could call in time of need, and which had been shunned by Isfandiyar: the Simurgh. The bird magically healed Rustam's wounds, and also revealed the only way in which Isfandiyar, who had been made invulnerable by Zoroaster, could be worsted: with a double-headed arrow made of the wood of the kazu tree, designed to pierce both his eyes simultaneously and blind him. He would thus be disabled but not killed, thereby averting catastrophe; for were he to die, the bird warned, his killer would not long survive him.

The next morning, Rustam made a last attempt to avert the tragedy that was unfolding, offering to go before Gushtasp so long as he could remain unfettered. But Isfandiyar refused. So battle began once more, and the old warrior fired the fatal arrow. It struck home, and the force of the blow not merely blinded the prince but also mortally wounded him.

Rustam did his best to succour the dying man, but to no avail. Yet before Isfandiyar passed away, the two heroes were reconciled, the prince even entrusting his surviving son to the good offices of his slayer. Then the end came; and so fate claimed a predestined victim and Persia lost its brightest star.

Isfandiyar waited until the Turanians had drunk their fill before massacring them all. This sword is from Persia, c.19th century.

99

The Death of Rustam

It was clear that Rustam's days upon the Earth would one day end. But when he did finally fall, it was not to the superior strength of a rival warrior but to treachery – and, most tragically of all, the plot was laid in the bosom of his own family.

The Simurgh had prophesied that Isfandiyar's killer would not long survive him, and its prediction soon proved accurate. Yet the way in which death finally came to Rustam would have been hard for the hero to foresee.

Without knowing it, he had incurred the hatred of his own half-brother Shughad, the son of Zal and a slave-girl. The younger man had been brought up in the royal household, and was now married to a daughter of the king of Kabul. Yet he remained envious of Rustam's reputation, and had long sought a way to humiliate or even kill him.

The king also resented his inferior status as a vassal of Sistan and hated Rustam for keeping him in subjection. One year when the annual tribute that Kabul had to pay was unexpectedly raised, his anger boiled over. In the presence of the younger man he spoke openly of revenge.

Shughad was only too eager to help. Between them, the two concocted a plan. First, though, they decided to lull any suspicions Rustam might have of their confederacy by staging a mock quarrel.

At a banquet in Kabul when the wine had flowed freely Shughad publicly insulted the king. The monarch responded furiously, calling his guest the son of a slave. This slur provided the pretext for Shughad to summon Rustam to defend the family honour. Hurrying to Sistan, he recounted the incident in exaggerated detail and begged his brother to help him take revenge.

Rustam at once agreed. The two brothers travelled back together to Kabul, where they were met by the king in person. Seemingly all repentance, he fell on his knees and begged the hero not to take offence at such a thoughtless remark.

Rustam was happy enough to accept such an abject apology, and thought it churlish to refuse when he was subsequently invited to stay on in Kabul for a few days' hunting – to cement the renewed friendship between the two royal families. In fact this invitation was the snare that the whole charade of anger and reconciliation had been designed to set. For the king had prepared man-traps along the route that the hunting party was to take; the road was pitted with deep holes lined on the bottom and sides with pointed stakes and

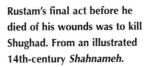

Rustam's final act before he died of his wounds was to kill Shughad. From an illustrated 14th-century *Shahnameh*.

blades. Yet from the road they were invisible, being carefully concealed under coverings of brushwood and flattened earth.

When the time came for the expedition, the king and Shughad were careful to let Rustam take the place of honour at the head of the procession on his faithful charger Rakhsh; seemingly to grant him due respect, they rode their own mounts safely behind him and to the side. When they reached the booby-trapped stretch, Rakhsh suddenly drew up of his own accord and refused to move on, no doubt sensing the smell of the disturbed earth and fearing some harm. For a moment it seemed as though the plotters' plan might be foiled. But Rustam, embarrassed by Rakhsh's unaccustomed stubbornness, gave the steed a mighty blow to the haunches, and Rakhsh leaped forward – straight into one of the pits.

Man and beast plunged together through the brushwood down onto the sharpened stakes below. Thrashing about in the darkness, they cut themselves repeatedly on the other blades projecting from the walls. Unable to fight back, they were both soon weak from the flow of blood that streamed from their many wounds.

Knowing they had been betrayed, Rustam cried out to his attackers for one last favour: to be given his bow, so that he could at least fight off any wild animals that came to torment him before he died. Before Shughad could stop him, an attendant threw down the weapon. Then, calling on his last reserves of strength, the old warrior dragged himself up the side of the pit, cutting himself further on the sword-blades as he did so. Seeing the danger, his brother fled for the safety of a nearby tree, seeking to take refuge behind its trunk. But Rustam saw where he had gone, and with a final, dying effort sent an arrow speeding after him that transfixed both the tree-trunk and the conspirator cowering behind it. Then, with the cold satisfaction of knowing that he had been avenged, Rustam fell back into the darkness. After sharing so many adventures over so long a time, he and Rakhsh died together. And all Persia mourned the death of the greatest hero the nation had ever known.

101

Sikander the World Conqueror

Alexander the Great features in the *Shahnameh* as Sikander, a bold young adventurer who conquers Iran along with much of the known world. But most of the tales the work tells of him owe more to poetic imagination than to reality.

The historical Alexander the Great was the son of Philip, the king of an area called Macedon, an outpost of Greek culture on the northern shores of the Aegean Sea. Tutored as a young man by the philosopher Aristotle, he inherited his father's throne when he was only nineteen and, after subduing the other Greek states, embarked on a plan to invade the mighty Persian empire that had originally been formulated by his father. He succeeded beyond his wildest dreams, conquering not just Persia itself and all its tributary states but also Egypt and the eastern Mediterranean lands. Not content to rest on his laurels, he then led his army eastwards through what would now be Afghanistan and Pakistan into northern India. His thirst for conquest was insatiable and his energy can only be marvelled at. He would have pressed on but when his men threatened rebellion he decided to turn back, returning to Babylon where he died of an infection at the age of just thirty-two.

As a Persian patriot, the *Shahnameh*'s author Firdowsi had obvious difficulties with this foreign conqueror of his homeland. In some places in the work he describes Sikander, as Alexander became known in Persia, as an enemy of Iran, as evil and destructive in his way as Afrasiab or serpent-shouldered Zahak. The poet particularly condemns his vandalism in destroying the Persian royal throne, a dynastic heirloom that successive monarchs had embellished over a long period of time.

Yet by the time he came to write the section of the epic that dealt specifically with Sikander's rule over Persia, his attitude had mellowed. He apparently had access to a Persian or Arabic translation of the best-known Greek life of Alexander, for his account reflects the story it tells though in idiosyncratic form, as if in a distorting mirror. And to the basic outline of the conqueror's life, as sketched above, Firdowsi added a

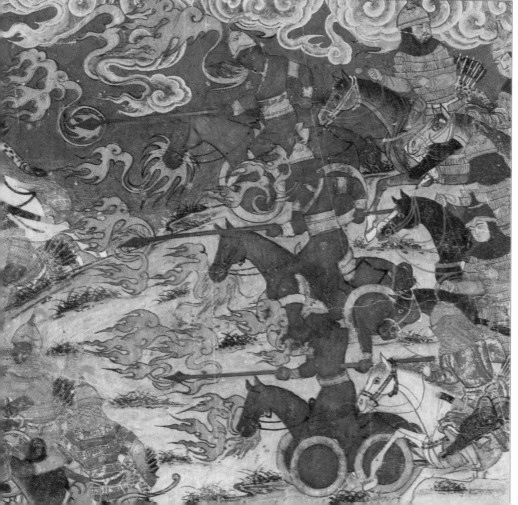

The awesome might of Alexander's conquering army is conjured by this miniature painting from Tabriz, *c.*1330. So great were the Greek prince's achievements that one Persian tradition claimed him as a hero of their own.

The Horned King

Persians call Alexander zulqarnain or "two-horned", reflecting an ancient historical misunderstanding.

Many explanations were given for the odd epithet, some drawing on other meanings of the Persian words involved. One, for instance, suggested that he wore his hair in plaits, for *qarn* can mean a lock of hair; another that on his travels he saw the dawn rise in both the east and west, for the same term can also mean the crescent of the rising sun.

In fact the real link seems to have been with the Egyptian god Amun, who was associated with rams. After conquering the country, Alexander followed established pharaonic practice by having himself portrayed as the god, complete with rams' horns. Seeing coins bearing this image, observers elsewhere in his far-flung empire evidently came to believe that the horns were his own.

Alexander is depicted with ram's horns on the face of this Thracian coin, c.3rd century BC.

number of travellers' tales and fantastic legends, no doubt inspired to do so by the real-life Alexander's taste for far-flung adventures.

The most serious problem confronting Firdowsi was the fact that Alexander had no known link to the Persian royal line. In the poet's scheme of things, that disqualified any claim he might have had to be a legitimate monarch, one marked out by the *farr*, the hereditary glory that adhered exclusively to the Iranian royal line; and without it, he could only be regarded as a usurper. So, to justify the relatively sympathetic treatment he accorded him, the poet resorted to deceit. He invented a connection where none actually existed, and he did so in a way that was deliberately unflattering to the Greeks.

In his version of events, the Persian emperor Darab waged successful war against the character Firdowsi calls Filicus, king of Rum – the term that Persians from the time of the Roman Empire onwards used promiscuously to refer to either Romans or Greeks; in this case, Philip of Macedon

was meant. When Filicus sued for peace, Darab graciously consented to grant it in return for an annual tribute of 100,000 golden eggs, each containing a precious jewel – and the hand of the Greek king's daughter, Nahid. But even though she was outstandingly beautiful, Nahid, it turned out, had bad breath. Persian physicians cured her of the complaint with the aid of a herbal infusion, but not before Darab, sickened by the odour, had determined to repudiate her. So he sent the girl back to her father, not knowing that he had already made her pregnant.

In time she bore a fine son, and her father Filicus, having no male offspring of his own, decided to adopt the boy as his heir. This was Sikander, the future world conqueror, who by Firdowsi's sleight of hand was thereby transformed into a scion of the Persian royal family.

Meanwhile, the poet continued, Darab had had another son by a second wife. Named Dara, he succeeded to the Persian throne on the death of his father. By that time Sikander had come to

103

power in Rum. But when Dara applied to him for the usual consignment of precious eggs, he refused to send it, choosing to go to war instead.

From that point onwards, Firdowsi's account of Sikander's career loosely follows the historical record. The warrior prince conquers Egypt and then wins two great victories over Dara's armies that make him master of Persia. Dara himself is forced to flee in the company of a dwindling band of followers, and is eventually killed by two of his own ministers, who hope thereby to ingratiate themselves with his conqueror. Firdowsi then takes the liberty of inserting a fictional death-bed meeting between Dara and Sikander, in which the new ruler promises to execute the assassins and to rule in accordance with established Persian custom. He then returns to his Greek sources to describe Sikander's progress eastwards to India, where he wins another great battle by using explosives to make his opponents' war-elephants panic.

Firdowsi enriches his account with a generous lacing of legend. He recounts an episode before Sikander's first confrontation with Dara, for instance, in which the invader goes in person to spy on the Persian camp in the guise of an envoy – and then has to flee for his life when he is eventually recognized, taking with him two golden cups belonging to the Persian king. Besides describing his real expedition to India, the *Shahnameh* also ascribes to him a series of fabulous journeys, to Andalusia, to the western ocean where the coastal-dwellers dress in women's clothing and only eat fish, and to a land of darkness beyond the sunset in which he searches for the Waters of Life.

Firdowsi's account also includes some prognostications of the conqueror's untimely death. One of the tales describes how Sikander visits a kingdom containing two talking trees, one male and one female. When he

consults them, they announce that he will never see Rum again but will die in Kashan, central Iran. Another premonition comes at a magic mountain guarded by a dragon, which Sikander slays; climbing the peak, he then finds at its summit the gorgeously attired corpse of a holy man while a disembodied voice tells him that his time is at hand.

Thereafter he journeys on to the city of Kashan, where he falls sick and dies a few days later, in accordance with the prophecy. In reality,

Alexander's death was followed by a division of his empire among his generals, with the Seleucids taking control of Iran (see box, page 17). As Firdowsi told the tale, however, Sikander's death was followed by a long period of anarchy when there was no Iranian-born King of Kings. "Two hundred years passed in this way," he claimed, "and it was as if there were no king in the world. You would have said the entire Earth enjoyed repose."

Persian Kings in the Old Testament

Tales from the Bible cast an interesting sidelight on early Persian history, offering valuable insights from the perspective of outsiders.

Persian history meets the Old Testament in the year 539BC, when Cyrus the Great defeated the last king of the Chaldean dynasty that had established the Neo-Babylonian Empire in Mesopotamia almost a hundred years before. The Chaldeans under Nebuchadrezzar had twice conquered the Jewish kingdom of Judah; on the second occasion in 586BC, the monarch had razed much of the city of Jerusalem and had forced many Jews into exile in the Babylonian Captivity.

For the Jews, then, the Persian takeover came as a liberation. Cyrus issued an edict permitting the expatriates to return to their native land, and many took the opportunity; their homecoming is chronicled in the Old Testament books of Ezra and Nehemiah. The emperor also allowed them to rebuild their temple in Jerusalem, which was undertaken in the reign of Darius, whose invasion of Greece ended at Marathon.

Some Jews continued in the service of the Persians, sometimes rising to senior positions. One such was the prophet Daniel. The story of his night in the lions' den tells how he was sentenced to the ordeal as a result of a plot by his enemies – and how delighted the Persian emperor for whom he worked was when he survived it unscathed. Another Jew who held high office under the Persians was Nehemiah, a palace servant of Artaxerxes I who was sent to Jerusalem for two periods of governorship during which he supervised the rebuilding of the city walls.

The events described in the Old Testament Book of Esther also took place against the backdrop of Persian rule. The story tells how Esther was chosen by Ahasuerus – Xerxes I (485–464BC) – to be his queen. Her frustration of an attempted pogrom of his Jewish subjects served to explain the origins of the secular thanksgiving feast of Purim, still celebrated today.

When Cyrus assumed power in Babylon in 539BC, he justified his actions in cuneiform script on this clay cylinder.

A Dream of Kingdoms

The last section of the *Shahnameh* is devoted to the Sasanian kings, who sought to restore the grandeur of the Persian empire of antiquity. Their founder was the warrior-monarch Ardashir whose forebears rose from the humblest of origins to fulfil their great destiny.

After the death of Sikander, the *Shahnameh* skips over more than half a millennium of Persian history. Firdowsi devotes only a few verses to the Parthian period, stretching from soon after the death of Alexander in 323BC until the establishment of the Sasanian dynasty in AD224, admitting that his sources revealed nothing of these rulers except their names.

Yet his concern with dynastic legitimacy remained. To cover the gap, he told the story of a son of Dara, the monarch whom Sikander supplanted. Supposedly the prince escaped to India and lived there in obscurity, starting a family that kept the royal bloodline alive over the generations, even though its scions were reduced to earning a living as shepherds or camel-drovers. The prince was called Sasan, and the name was passed down to all the eldest sons of the line.

Eventually one of them went to work for a rich man called Babak, in time becoming his head shepherd. One night Babak had a dream in which he saw Sasan seated on an elephant receiving the salutations of a multitude of people. When, twenty-four hours later, he had another night-time vision of Sasan surrounded by sacred fires, he sent for wise men who could tell him what the dreams might mean. The sages advised him that they signified that either Sasan himself or else his heir would one day rule the world.

Delighted by the news, Babak loaded the surprised shepherd with riches and gave him his own daughter in marriage. In time, the couple had a son they named Ardashir. He was expensively educated by his doting grandfather and grew up to be the very model of a young nobleman. Summoned to court, he quickly won favour with the Parthian emperor Ardavan.

But Ardashir had the pride of a prince, and he lost the ruler's goodwill when he one day accused one of the emperor's own sons of lying in the course of a dispute on the hunting-field. As punishment for his impudence, he was reduced to a lowly position as a royal stablehand.

Ardashir's Revenge

The unexpected demotion left Ardashir bitterly angry with the court and its ruler. His disaffection received fresh focus when he happened to attract the amorous attention of the king's favourite concubine, a slave-girl named Golnar who was also a trusted adviser of the monarch. The two secretly became lovers – and so Ardashir was the first to know when Ardavan received an undisclosed communication from his astrologers informing him that he would one day lose his coveted throne to the youth he had disgraced.

Fearing Ardavan's response, the couple took pre-emptive action. Golnar raided the royal treasury, to which she had privileged access, and the two fled from court with as much wealth as they could carry away with them.

As it happened, the Parthian king was widely unpopular at the time. So when news of Ardashir's defection spread, warriors came from near and far to rally to his cause. Before long he had an army behind him. With it he defeated first Ardavan's son and then the emperor himself, who was killed on the battlefield.

Ardavan's death paved the way for Ardashir to claim the throne. Marrying the former ruler's daughter to further legitimize his claim and unify potentially hostile factions, Ardashir had himself crowned King of Kings at Ctesiphon, near

Baghdad, and went on to reign as gloriously as any of the former monarchs; "no one could distinguish him from Gushtasp," Firdowsi claimed.

And at that point, with Ardashir's rise to power, the legendary section of the *Shahnameh* comes to an end. Though the work tracks the history of the Persian kings for a further 400 years, it sticks relatively closely to the historical record, which by that stage was much fuller than for earlier years; Firdowsi was able to consult chronicles prepared for the Sasanian rulers themselves, who were both patrons of learning and concerned with their own place in Iranian history.

In fact, their ascendancy provided a fitting conclusion for the work, for in a sense it was their legacy that Firdowsi had devoted his life's work to

perpetuating. Like them, he saw Persian history as a continuum linked by the high deeds of its kings. And he also followed in their footsteps in viewing the heroic past as the touchstone of national identity. The Sasanians tried to reawaken the glories of the Achaemenian kings just as Firdowsi consciously enumerated the doings of Rustam, Kay Khusrow and Isfandiyar and the like with a view to inspiring future generations by their example. And given the lasting popularity of the work among Persians of all classes, it is clear that he succeeded more fully than he could ever have hoped.

The investiture of the Sasanian king Ardashir II (AD379–383), carved into the rocks at Tagh-e Bostan. Mithra, with the barsom twigs, and Ahura Mazda, give their blessing to his rule.

MAGIC FROM THE SKY

High up in the Alburz Mountains lived one of the most mysterious creatures in Persian mythology: the Simurgh. It descended at crucial moments in the *Shahnameh* to offer mortals magic that could save their lives – rescuing Zal, helping at the birth of Rustam and later telling him how to slay Isfandiyar – but its origins remain as obscure as its motives. It was probably derived from the Saena or Senmurv, the great falcon that nested on the Tree of Many Seeds (see page 29), while some have even linked it to Verethragna's guise as an auspicious raven (see page 32). What is clear, however, is that the Simurgh made a dramatic impression on generations of artists as the colourful and exotic king of the birds.

Above: Birds held a particular fascination for the Persians from ancient times. The griffin, giant images of which towered over the city of Persepolis, was as recurrent a theme in Achaemenian art as the sphinx was in Egyptian. The Rokh of the Sinbad stories was another avian beast – but one which seldom proved auspicious. This exotic bronze bird is from Khorasan, northeastern Persia, *c.*10th–11th century.

Left: The Simurgh was a favourite motif of the Sasanians for whom the creature was half-dog, half-bird, as shown on this 7th–8th century silver-gilt plate. In post-Islamic times, the Simurgh lost its canine associations and was depicted solely as a creature of the sky.

Above: The Simurgh's influence spread
beyond Persia's own borders. It has
been linked with Simargl, Slav god of
seed and new shoots, while its fabulous
tail-feathers also recall the Firebird of
Russian folklore. This illustration is
from an 18th-century *Shahnameh* from
Kashmir, showing the Simurgh carrying
Zal to its nest in the Alburz Mountains.

Left: A late-Sasanian stucco plaque of
the Simurgh from Ray, south of Tehran,
*c.*7th–8th century. The prevalence of
such images on everyday items, like
fabrics, dishes and on stucco, confirms
the talismanic nature of the bird that
Isfandiyar foolishly killed (see page 98).

LAND OF THE STORY-TELLERS

After the Arab conquest of Persia in AD633–651, the divine beings of Zoroastrianism were forced underground by the new faith of Islam. But like the Celtic deities of Ireland after the coming of Christianity, they did not disappear completely and eventually resurfaced in folklore as the *peri* and *div* of later Iranian tradition.

They were far from the only marvellous characters to populate the wonder tales in which the nation delighted. Peopled with giants, enchanters, beautiful princesses and fearsome monsters, these elaborate fantasies often took the form of epic quests in which the hero or heroine had to perform some magical task in order to win true love. For the most part the stories were passed down by word of mouth, for poets and chroniclers preferred to reserve their efforts for the high deeds of kings and warriors.

One way in which they were transmitted was by professional story-tellers, the *naqqal*. Mostly these men specialized in telling tales from the *Shahnameh*, but they also often developed a sideline in folktales. Nineteenth-century travellers described them as picturesque figures wearing skull-caps and short trousers of animal hide, waving huge clubs or axes to emphasize points or as props to act out dramatic moments; one sub-group, the *pardehdar*, illustrated the stories in a literal sense, with painted backdrops on which key episodes of the story were depicted. By that time the story-tellers had been organized into a guild; its chief officer was a court official entrusted with the job of telling stories to the shah each evening until he fell asleep.

In time, the tale-telling tradition was to create some great literature in its own right. Poets such as Gurgani and Nizami (see page 131) composed epics of courtly love that paralleled the Arthurian romances popular at the time in Europe. Yet the wonder tales were to have their own monument too, for the best found their way into the great compendium of stories from all over the Middle East and India, the *Thousand and One Nights*. This collection of fantastic tales proved an enormous international success – so much so that the stories became part of the heritage not just of Persia but of the whole world.

Opposite: **Zamarrad the giant is attacked by guards in a scene from the *Hamzanameh*, or "Romance of Amir Hamza", c.1570.**

Below: **This gold armlet, from the Oxus hoard c.5th–4th century BC, is decorated with griffins, Persia's best-known mythical beasts.**

The Book of 1,000 Tales

The tale of Shehrezad that frames the *Thousand and One Nights* is one of the world's most celebrated stories. Less well-known is the fact that it came from an earlier Persian work that gave its name to the entire collection.

The story tells of two brothers of the Sasanian dynasty, the elder of whom, Shahriyar, ruled over India and China while the younger, Shahzaman, was king of Samarkand. To their horror, both men learned that their wives had been unfaithful to them. But Shahriyar actually saw his wife joining in an orgy with slaves and serving-girls.

Deranged by the experience and convinced of the deceitfulness of all women, the vengeful monarch took drastic measures. He had his wife killed on the spot and then announced his intention of marrying a new bride every day, only to have her executed at dawn the following morning.

For three years Shahriyar lived up to his bloodthirsty pledge, until his realm eventually began to run out of suitable young women. Charged with the job of finding fresh candidates, his vizir was at his wits' end when Shehrezad, his own daughter, offered herself for the post. Her father tried to dissuade her but Shehrezad had a plan and she insisted on putting it into operation.

While the story of Shehrezad works as a cunning narrative device, many Persians made their own living from reciting tales. This painting of story-tellers is attributed to Jani, 1684–5.

The Origins of the
Thousand and One Nights

Although the prologue to the Thousand and One Nights *itself* **speaks of its debt to a "Persian book", the tales it contains in fact came from all over the Middle East and India, and even echoed stories in the Bible and Greek mythology.**

Detail from a 13th-century manuscript attributed to Abou Ma'Schar. Scribes helped to disseminate the many stories.

Textual analysis provides scant clues to the origins of the *Thousand and One Nights* for, apart from a single page dating from the tenth century, the earliest surviving manuscript was put together in Syria in the fourteenth or fifteenth century. The stories, however, are much older and scholars agree that most came from India, Persia, Mesopotamia, the Arab lands and Egypt.

Yet the story-tellers' stock-in-trade recognized no frontiers, taking in tales from other cultures too. Many critics have pointed out the similarities between Sinbad's encounter with a giant on his third voyage with Ulysses's escape from Polyphemus in Homer's *Odyssey*. And the tale of "The Devout Woman and the Two Wicked Elders" is essentially the same as that of Susannah and the Elders in the Apocrypha to the Hebrew Old Testament.

And the tales could span millennia as well as national boundaries. There are echoes in the *Nights* of the "Tale of the Shipwrecked Sailor" from ancient Egypt and even, in "The Adventures of Bulukiyya", of the quest for immortality described in the Babylonian *Epic of Gilgamesh*, believed to date back as far as 2100BC.

Her scheme employed her exceptional skills as a story-teller. She counted on whiling away the wedding night with a tale she would leave unfinished at dawn the following morning. The king, she hoped, would be so eager to know the outcome that he would postpone her beheading.

The stratagem worked, for when dawn broke, Shahriyar was desperate to learn the end of the story and duly ordered a stay of execution. Shehrezad continued in the same manner for a total of 1,000 nights, in the course of which she also bore the ruler three sons.

On the thousand and first night she finally ran out of stories. Then, parading the children before the ruler, she cast herself on his mercy. With tears in his eyes, he told her that he had long since made the decision to pardon her, for he sincerely loved her. And the work ends happily amid public celebrations.

Evidence that this memorable tale had Persian origins comes from a 10th-century Arab chronicler named al-Masoudi who wrote of a book from that country named *Hazar Afsanah* ("A Thousand Legends"). Evidence within the story itself also suggests a Persian origin, notably the reference to Sasanian kings and the unmistakably Iranian names of the characters.

Even so, the origins of the tales as a whole are eclectic, and the Iranian influence is only one among many. The work has been compared to an ocean of stories; with the Persian contribution just one of the major streams that went to fill it.

The Quest for a Distant Lover

One popular form of Persian folktale concerned men who fell in love with girls in far-off lands whom they had never met. In the tale of Seif al-Muluk, the search for an elusive lover becomes an epic quest spanning much of the then-known world.

Sailors watch in fear and wonder as a mysterious sea monster swims beneath their boat, in a 16th-century Mughal miniature painting. Amid the dry plains of Persia, tales of seafaring to strange and distant lands held a particular fascination.

The story of "Seif al-Muluk" is an ancient one, known to have been in circulation by the mid-11th century AD. Evidence of its popularity in the Middle East comes in the *Thousand and One Nights* tale immediately preceding it. This tells how a Persian ruler offered a huge reward to anyone who could find the most marvellous story ever invented. That tale turned out to be none other than "Seif al-Muluk", which an envoy heard from a story-teller in the marketplace of Damascus. The king was so delighted with it that he had it inscribed in his treasury in letters of gold.

The tale describes how Seif fell in love with Princess Badiyeh after seeing her portrait on a magic tunic. From it he learned that her father was a king of the *jinns,* or genies – powerful spirits – and that they lived in the city of Babel. No one knew where Babel was, so Seif set off to find it.

First he travelled to China, but without success. Next he tried the Indian Ocean, whose islands provided the setting for a series of fantastic adventures. On one, an Old Man of the Sea like the one in the better-known "Sinbad" story leaped onto one of his companion's backs and could not be removed; on another, the sailors were attacked by monstrous creatures whose ears were so big they wrapped themselves up in them to go to sleep. On a third they fell into the hands of cannibalistic giants who put Seif and three shipmates in cages, mistaking them for exotic birds.

When the four eventually escaped by raft, it was only for Seif to see his companions eaten by giant crocodiles. Alone, he next landed on an island of apes, where he was invited to remain as king. Eventually he fetched up at the palace of a foster-sister of Badiyeh, whom he rescued from the clutches of a hostile *jinn,* the son of the Blue King, who had imprisoned her. She subsequently helped him in his quest, taking him to the capital of her father, the king of Hind, and using magic to make Princess Badiyeh appear before him.

Badiyeh fell in love with her handsome suitor, but there remained the problem of gaining parental approval for a match that spanned the spirit and human worlds. By following the princess's advice, Seif won the support of her grandmother, who pleaded his cause with her son.

Yet Seif's troubles were still far from over. Spirited away from his beloved's garden by agents of the Blue King, he was thrown into prison and only rescued when Princess Badiyeh's father threatened to declare war to win his release. Then at last the two lovers were finally reunited, and at the same time his vizir, the faithful companion for much of his travels, was married to Badiyeh's foster-sister. And the two couples lived happily for the rest of their days.

The Goldsmith and the Singing Girl

Another tale about Persia concerning a romantic quest tells of a lovesick goldsmith who lost his heart to a painted image.

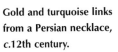

Gold and turquoise links from a Persian necklace, c.12th century.

A goldsmith once saw the girl of his dreams painted on the wall of a friend's house, and discovered from the painter that the model was a singing girl in the harem of a vizir of the king of Kashmir. Travelling to India, he soon learned where she lived, along with news of a peculiarity of the king – that he lived in fear of sorcery and regularly left suspected witches to starve to death in a pit outside the city walls.

The goldsmith decided to put the knowledge to good use. Breaking into the vizir's palace, he made no attempt to abduct the girl but instead nicked her in the thigh with a knife and took her jewel casket. Then, craving an audience with the king, he presented him with the gems, claiming he had been attacked

by witches outside the city gate and had fought them off, wounding one on the thigh. Fleeing, the sorceress had left the jewel-box behind her and he wished to give it as a gift to the kind monarch.

Rummaging through its contents, the king found jewels he had given his vizir, who quickly identified the present owner as the singing girl. Summoned, she was found to have a wound exactly where the scholar had described. The king needed no further proof of her guilt. He sentenced her to be thrown into the punishment pit just as the goldsmith had known he would. For it was then an easy matter for the suitor to bribe the pit's guard and head off with his beloved to a happy new life in far-off Persia.

Weaving Tales of Wonder

One of the most distinctive literary devices of the *Thousand and One Nights* is the story within a story – a technique used throughout the work to create narrative patterns as complex as the designs in a Persian carpet.

Stories within stories were a familiar device in Persian literature from an early time. In the *Thousand and One Nights*, the stratagem suits the basic premise of the work, providing Shehrezad with an easy way of stringing out tales to avoid reaching a conclusion, thereby putting off the evil moment of her execution. It also allowed story-tellers themselves to link tales that shared common elements but also had important differences.

There are many sequences, one of which groups the tales told by seven vizirs. The premise is that a young prince, his father's only son, is forced to remain silent for a week, a sage having predicted that harm would come to him if he spoke during that time. He is sent to his father's harem as a supposedly safe refuge but he has the misfortune to attract the amorous attention of the king's favourite concubine. When he rejects her advances she gets her revenge by telling the monarch that the young man tried to violate her. Enraged, the ruler orders his immediate execution. But his seven vizirs fear that he will later change his mind and punish them if they carry out the command, so they seek to delay the fateful moment by telling stories on the general theme of the unreliability of women. The concubine tries to counter their ploy by herself telling tales depicting the male sex in a bad light.

Some of the tales show an ingenuity in plot elaboration that would do credit to a French farce. One describes how a libertine, seeking to seduce a chaste wife whose husband has gone away on business, turns for help to a bawd. The older woman ingratiates herself with the intended victim, and then one day shows her a bitch whose eyes she has caused to water by feeding it a cake flavoured with pepper. The wife asks why the animal is crying, and the crone tells her that it is really no dog but a beautiful young woman who has been bewitched for refusing to take a lover.

Terrified that the same fate might befall her too, the wife agrees to give herself to the man who has been pursuing her. But at the crucial moment he cannot be found, and the bawd, unwilling to lose the money she had been promised, instead approaches a travel-stained stranger she sees in the street, in the hope that he will agree to pay her for the deceived wife's favours. The man agrees to go to meet the young woman and is horrified to find that he is being led to his own house, for as luck would have it he is the wife's husband newly returned from his travels. But the wife, seeing him coming and thinking quickly, turns a potentially disastrous situation to her own advantage by pummelling him furiously as he enters the building. So, she says, he has fallen into the trap she had laid for him: now she knows for sure that he frequents loose women!

The parade of stories finally comes to an end on the eighth day, when the prince is at last free to speak and so to proclaim his probity. The cycle ends happily, for the young man displays his wisdom with a sequence of exemplary tales of his own, then successfully begs for forgiveness for the erring concubine. Completely won over, the old king agrees merely to send her away and to abdicate in favour of the son who has so successfully demonstrated his magnanimity as well as his innocence of the charge laid against him.

The intricate designs and interweaving of traditional Persian carpets, typified by this silk and wool rug from Isfahan in central Iran, reflect a delight in complexity which is found also in indigenous narrative forms.

Prince Ahmed and the Peri *Banu*

Wealthy, beautiful and immortal, *peri* were the fairies of Persian folklore and like their counterparts in Celtic myth they lived in an alternative world hidden very close to the human one. Communication between the two, however, was seldom free from trouble.

Once an ageing sultan had three sons and a beautiful niece, Nuronihar, whom all three wished to marry. The ruler declared that the girl would marry the one who went off into the world and came back with the greatest marvel.

After a year, the three brothers met up to compare their discoveries. The eldest had a magic carpet; the middle brother had found a tube

through which the viewer could see whatever sight he wanted; and the youngest, Ahmed, had an apple that could heal the worst sickness.

Testing the finds, one of the princes used the tube to spy on Nuronihar and was horrified to see she lay mortally ill. At once the three determined to help her. The magic carpet took them to her in a flash, and the apple made her well again.

But their very success created a dilemma for their father, who pointed out that all three possessions had been equally essential for her recovery. So he suggested as a tie-breaker a competition to see who could fire an arrow the farthest.

The brothers sent their arrows winging into the distance, but Ahmed's went so far that it disappeared from sight. He was disqualified, and the hand of Nuronihar went to the middle brother.

Crushed by this cruel twist of fate, Ahmed set off disconsolately in the direction the arrow had taken. After some hours he was amazed to find the errant shaft at the foot of a small hill, well beyond the range of any human bowman. Gazing around, he noted an iron door that opened into an enchanted realm of shining jewels. This was the home of Banu, a fairy princess.

Ahmed quickly learned that Banu had carried his arrow to the threshold of her palace for, she readily confessed, she loved him. Forgetting Nuronihar in the radiance of Banu's beauty, Ahmed readily consented to stay with the princess in her underground treasure-chamber.

When Ahmed's bolt disappeared from sight, he was disqualified from the challenge set by his father. But his curiosity drove him to follow the arrow's flight, leading him to the beautiful *peri* Banu. This archer is from a 17th-century Mughal miniature.

They lived there happily for some months, but eventually Ahmed grew restless to see his father. Fearing danger, Banu tried to persuade him not to go, for she knew that contacts between the human and spirit worlds rarely ended happily.

Ahmed insisted, and the first visits went well. But before long the sultan, eager to know his son's secrets, turned to a sorceress, who poisoned his mind against his son. Learning of the prince's supernatural connection, she suggested putting it to use by setting him impossible tasks. So he was asked first for a tent small enough to carry in a man's hand yet large enough when opened to shelter an entire army, and then for a vial of water from a fountain that cured all ills.

With Banu's aid Ahmed completed both tasks, but his father asked for a third marvel: a man the height of a footstool with a beard twenty times longer than he was, carrying an iron rod weighing a quarter of a ton.

Ahmed was at a loss, but Banu revealed that this odd being was her own brother, a mighty *jinn* called Schaibar. He proved only too willing to help his sister's friend, but set about doing so in his own way – killing the king and all his counsellors, as well as the evil sorceress. Then he got the cowering survivors to set Ahmed on the throne, with Banu as his queen. No one disputed the proposal; and Ahmed and Banu ruled the kingdom wisely for many long years.

From Furies to Fairies

Persia's fairy princesses, peri, *were beautiful female spirits said to live in enchanted palaces, feeding only on the sweetest perfumes. Yet their origins were altogether much less inviting.*

Scholars have traced *peri's* ancestry back to the *pairaka* of the *Avesta*, witch-like spirits who transformed themselves into beautiful maidens to lead men astray. When the old religion was supplanted by Islam, these unappetizing hags underwent a remarkable transformation, resurfacing in folklore with their sinister aspects suppressed and only the good remaining.

In later times, *peri* were thought of as benevolent beings formed exclusively of the element of fire. Orthodox Muslims explained them away as descendants of the fallen angels, and as such neither human nor divine. They had their maleficent equivalent in the *div*, spirits of darkness who persecuted them endlessly; one of their favourite tricks was to imprison captured *peri* in iron cages suspended high up in trees.

The *Avesta* described wicked spirits who beguiled men by appearing as beautiful maidens. In later folktales, these sprites became benevolent fairies, seen here entertaining a prince in a Persian miniature painting, *c.*16th century.

The Envious Sisters

A relatively late addition to the *Thousand and One Nights*, this typical Persian wonder tale describes the victimization and redemption of a blameless queen in a magical narrative spanning two generations.

Although the tale of the "Envious Sisters" appeared in the first Western translation of the *Thousand and One Nights*, made by the Frenchman Antoine Galland in the early 1700s, it did not feature in the Arab manuscript from which he worked. It seems that he heard the story from a Christian Arab named Hanna Diab who was in Paris at the time, and who also provided him with such familiar tales as "Aladdin" and "Ali Baba".

This sultan liked to wander the streets of his capital in disguise, and while doing so one evening he overheard a dispute between three sisters. One said she dreamed of marrying the sultan's baker, the second his chief cook, but the third and youngest said that she would like to marry the sultan himself. He was so amused by the incident, that he decided to grant them their respective wishes, and ordered his vizir to arrange the three weddings at once.

The youngest girl proved to be an excellent wife, and in due course bore the ruler a fine and healthy son. But her two elder sisters were consumed with jealousy at her superior station and decided to take a cruel revenge. They stole away with the baby as it slept in its cradle and set it afloat on a canal near the palace. They then told the sultan that his wife had given birth not to a human baby but to a puppy instead.

Twice more the queen became pregnant, but each time the wicked sisters repeated the same trick. Eventually the sultan lost patience with this wife who repeatedly bore monsters and decided to rid himself of her. He ordered that she should be imprisoned in a specially constructed box outside the gateway of his capital's principal mosque and that the faithful should spit on her each time they entered or left the building.

The sisters thought that their triumph was complete, but they did not know that the three discarded children had been rescued by a court official who lived along the canal on which they had

Two princesses walk amid flowering fruit and cypress trees in a luxurious Persian garden, miniature painting, c.1558.

been abandoned. Two boys and a girl, they were welcomed into his household as the heirs he and his wife had always longed for.

When the three grew up, the functionary installed them in a large estate outside the capital which they duly inherited on his death. The boys, young men now, spent their time hunting, and while they were out one day the girl, Parizad, invited an old Muslim woman in to make her devotions. The guest complimented her on the beauties of the estate, but said that it lacked three things to make it perfect: the Talking Bird, the Singing Tree and the Golden Water. Parizad asked where these marvels could be found, and the woman told her that they lay far away on the borders of India.

Parizad's brothers at once decided to go in search of them, but the route proved dangerous. It led to an ancient dervish whose hair reached to his feet. When the elder brother arrived, this man directed him to a nearby mountain where, he said, he would find the objects of his quest. But at its foot lay great piles of black stones. He must pass through these without looking to left or right, even though he might hear voices calling out to him, trying to distract him.

The prince did his best to heed the man's advice, but as he passed the mysterious black rocks he heard strange cries of anguish and could not help glancing to one side. As he did so, he was instantly turned to stone himself. Soon afterwards the same misfortune befell his younger brother. It was left to Parizad to succeed where they had failed and to bring back the wonders from the mountaintop; and on her way down she was able to restore her brothers and all the other stones to life by sprinkling them with drops of the magical Golden Water.

In due course the sultan heard of the marvels and requested to see them. He was mightily impressed by all three objects, and especially by

the Golden Water, a mere drop of which was enough to create a magnificent fountain. He was also startled by the lunch he was served, whose centrepiece was a cucumber that Parizad had stuffed with pearls. She had done this at the suggestion of the Talking Bird, a wise fowl with an ulterior motive in mind. For when the ruler commented that he had never seen such a sight before, the cunning bird chipped in by asking if it was really any odder than the notion of a wife bringing forth three monsters.

Having won the sultan's undivided attention, the magic fowl then went on to reveal the true identity of his three hosts and the injustice that had been done so many years before. In the wake of the revelations, mother and children were reunited and the wife was restored to her former state. The two envious sisters were then forced to confess their wrong-doing and were instantly done to death for the harm they had caused.

A bronze incense burner, from Khorasan in northeast Persia, *c.*12th century. It took a strange talking bird to make the sultan see the intrigues that had robbed him of his wife and children.

The Captured Bride

The curious tale of Hasan of Basra illustrates two aspects of later Persian legend as reflected in the *Thousand and One Nights*: the recurring theme of a captured bride, and the transformation of the old Zoroastrian priesthood in the popular imagination into the sorcerers and villains of traditional legend.

The story featuring Hasan of Basra is a fairytale epic that combines all the ingredients of a classic *Thousand and One Nights* tale. It tells of sorcerers, abductions, magical islands, princesses in faraway castles and a heroine saved from execution. The protagonist is a merchant from the port city of Basra on the Persian Gulf. His adventures in search of wealth and love form the linking theme, while travellers' tales told by real-life merchants trading out into the Indian Ocean evidently provided the inspiration for its far-flung settings.

The story recounts that Hasan was a goldsmith, visited one day in his stall in Basra's bazaar by a mysterious stranger. The newcomer, a Persian, claimed to be able to transmute copper into gold, and gave Hasan a convincing demonstration of his alchemical powers. He turned out to be a fire-worshipping magus, a relic of the old Zoroastrian priesthood, transformed in the popular imagination after the coming of Islam into an evil magician. Worse still, it transpired that to work his magic he had to kill a Muslim annually, and Hasan was that year's chosen victim.

So Hasan found himself drugged and abducted on board ship, bound he knew not where. When the magician made a landfall to find a herb necessary for his alchemical spells, Hasan escaped and fled into the wilderness. After some time, exhausted and hungry, he stumbled upon an isolated palace where seven princesses had been secluded by their father. Glad of male company, they kept him for a whole year, at the end of which their father arrived to take them off to attend a marriage feast.

They had kept Hasan hidden for fear their parent might punish them, and when they left for the wedding they gave Hasan the freedom of the palace, but with one proviso: he was not to enter a locked room whose secret they refused to reveal.

Hasan's curiosity was aroused and, needless to say, he very soon disobeyed their instructions. He made his way to the far corner of the palace

When Hasan met the alchemist he was amazed by his ability to turn copper into gold – but terrified of his dark intentions. This golden head comes from northeast Persia, 5th–4th century BC.

A detail from a Persian miniature, *c.*1480. Disguised as birds, *peri* could fly wherever they wished. But when Hasan stole the feathers of his beloved she was left stranded at his mercy.

The pair stayed for a time with the princesses in their palace, and the bird-wife bore Hasan two children. But Hasan eventually grew homesick and determined to journey to Basra to see his long-lost mother. Promising the princesses that he would come back, he set off with his wife and family and arrived safely at his destination. His mother was overjoyed to see him, having long thought him dead, and the extended family enjoyed the happiest of reunions.

When the time came for Hasan to revisit the princesses, he left his family with his mother, revealing his wife's secret to her and giving her strict instructions to keep her feather outfit carefully hidden. But the wife succeeded in outwitting her mother-in-law and, donning the feathers, immediately turned into a bird and flew off, with the children enfolded in her plumage. As she left, she shouted that if Hasan ever wanted to see her again he would find her on the islands of Wak-Wak. Then she disappeared into the distance.

So once more Hasan, heartbroken at his loss, had to set off on his travels. With the aid of the seven princesses and of their uncle, a kindly enchanter, he eventually succeeded in finding the islands. There, after many adventures in which his wife was nearly done to death by a cruel sister only to be rescued by Hasan with the aid of a magic wand and a cap of invisibility, the couple managed to escape to the Mountain of Clouds. Travelling on to Baghdad, they settled down happily with Hasan's mother, and the *peri,* reconciled to her life among mortals, put away for ever all thoughts of donning her feathers again.

With its enchanters, fairy princesses, impossible journeys and erotic fantasies, Hasan's story is typical of the *samar,* tales of the evening told to beguile the leisure hours after the working day was done. Its episodic structure and all-action plotline reflect the demands of the professional story-tellers, who needed a constant flow of wonders to keep their audience entertained.

and tried the forbidden door. It was unlocked and when he opened it he found himself at the foot of a tall and winding staircase which led him to a splendid roof-garden. There he saw a group of fairy-like maidens bathing in a pool. One glimpse was all it took for him to fall in love with the most beautiful girl among them.

When the princesses returned, they noticed Hasan's distracted state and immediately guessed what had happened. They revealed to him that his beloved was a *peri* (see page 119), the daughter of a king of the *jinn,* who came to the pool once every month at the time of the new moon.

Hasan determined to meet her once again and when the appointed hour next came round, he was ready and waiting. Amazed, he saw the girls descend onto the roof in the form of a flock of birds. When they took human shape to go bathing, he stole out and hid his love's precious feathers, depriving her of the chance to escape. When the others took their leave, she was stranded and Hasan appeared before her protesting his love. Eventually, after much persuasion, she agreed to marry him.

The Minstrel Tradition

Minstrels were a fixture of Persian court life many centuries before they became familiar in the West. Their legacy of songs and stories eventually bore literary fruit in courtly romances that had parallels with the Arthurian legends of medieval Europe.

The minstrel tradition went back a long way in Persia. In the fourth century BC, a Greek traveller, Chares of Mytilene, is said to have heard Persians singing the romance of Zariadres and Odatis, retold in the *Shahnameh* 1,300 years later. The great Sasanian ruler Bahram V (known as Bahram Gur), who reigned in the fifth century AD, numbered among his favourites a Greek slave-girl who sang tales to a harp accompaniment and who frequently accompanied him on hunting expeditions. The same king reputedly once asked an Indian emperor to send him 10,000 male and female musicians together with their instruments.

Many of the minstrels simply performed traditional songs and lays, but there were others who composed their own material. One such was Rudaki, hailed before his death in AD940 as the "king of the poets" and still recognized as the first great writer in the modern Persian tongue. Like the Homer of tradition, he was probably blind, and sang his songs to the strains of the harp or lute.

Minstrels who played for the king and his court were known as *ramishgar* or *khuniyagar*, and there was stiff competition for the post, as the story of Barbad shows (see box, opposite). The songs they sang were mostly about love, and they encouraged a lyrical tradition of courtly romance that had a marked influence on Persian literature.

The first great example was the story of Vis and Ramin as described by the poet Gurgani, written in about AD1050. At the time the Seljuk Turks were conquering Persia, and Gurgani's poem was dedicated to the governor of Isfahan, a Seljuk appointee. His work was apparently based on an earlier version of the tale written in Sasanian times. Gurgani's patron ordered him to "Beautify this story as April does the garden".

Early poets would have been minstrels, singing their own and others' creations to whoever would listen to them. Here musicians play on a *nava*, from a 15th-century manuscript.

According to Gurgani's version, Mubad Manikan, king of Marv in what is now Turkmenistan on Iran's northeastern frontier, fell in love with Shahru, queen of Mah – the ancient country of the Medes in western Persia. She rejected his advances, pointing out that she was already married and had a son, Viru. The persistent Mubad, however, would not take no for an answer, and made her promise, on oath and in writing, that if she were ever to bear a daughter she would give her to him as his wife.

When she made the promise Shahru thought herself too old to have another child, but to her surprise she subsequently did bear a baby girl, whom she named Vis. The infant was put in the care of a wetnurse who took her to her own home

Barbad the "Invisible" Musician

The Shahnameh *describes the cunning ruse employed by one minstrel to win the coveted position of chief singer to the king.*

The Sasanian monarch Khusrow II Parviz (see page 130) was a great patron of the arts. Word of his munificence reached Barbad, a talented musician who was inspired to seek his fortune at court. But when he arrived he was disappointed to learn that the king already had an official minstrel, named Sarkash.

Having heard Sarkash sing, Barbad knew his own talent was greater, but could think of no way of displaying his abilities to the monarch. Eventually he befriended one of the royal gardeners and devised a plan. Dressed entirely in green he was smuggled into the gardens and concealed himself in a tree just before Khusrow was due to visit. When the royal party arrived, he played and sang so sweetly from his hiding-place in the branches that all the guests stopped stock-still and listened open-mouthed. Ravished, the monarch offered to fill the lap of the unseen songster with gems if only he would step forward and reveal his identity.

Barbad climbed down and paid his humblest respects to the king, telling him that he was his devoted slave and his only wish in life was to sing for him.

The stratagem worked and from that day on he duly supplanted Sarkash in the royal favour and in the course of time won lasting fame as the greatest of all court minstrels.

in the region of Khuzestan, by the Persian Gulf. As chance would have it, the nurse was also rearing Ramin, the infant brother of Mubad. So the two children grew up in each others' company before being sent back to their respective parents when they reached adolescence.

By then Vis had grown into such a beauty that her mother decided that only one man was worthy to wed her: her own brother Viru. And so the two siblings were married in a splendid ceremony. But the festivities were marred when Zard, Mubad's half-brother, arrived to remind Shahru of her long-forgotten promise. When Vis refused to contemplate leaving Viru, Mubad in his wrath determined to go to war to reclaim what he regarded as his due.

The two opposing forces both enlisted the aid of allies, Mubad turning to the eastern powers and Viru to those of western Persia. When the armies finally met, Mubad's men were defeated, though not before Viru's own father, a famous warrior, had been killed. But Viru was not able to follow up his victory, for other enemies threatened his kingdom from the north. Profiting from his distraction, Mubad diverted his retreating troops to the castle where Shahru and Vis were sheltering. There he finally persuaded Shahru to surrender Vis, first by reminding her of the oath she had sworn before God and then by showering her with rich gifts. Triumphantly he rode off to Marv with his prize.

In fact he was only storing up troubles to come. First, Ramin caught sight of the princess on the journey, and at once fell passionately in love with her. He found an ally in his old nurse, who now hurried to Marv to share the company of her two former charges. Like her counterpart in *Romeo and Juliet*, she was to play an important role in the chain of events that followed. For she had powers as a sorceress, and at Vis's behest she used them to make the old king impotent. At the same time, she was persuaded by Ramin to act as a go-between with Vis, arranging an assignation between the two lovers.

From that initial deception followed a pattern of passionate attachment, jealousy and betrayal. Three times the lovers eloped from Mubad's court, but each time Vis ended up back with her hated husband. Driven almost mad by jealousy, the king still could not bring himself to do away with either his brother or the woman he doted on. Instead, he tried to shelter Vis from Ramin, but all his attempts to sequester her ended in failure.

Things finally came to a head at a court banquet when a minstrel sang a song that elliptically referred to the love of Vis and Ramin. The king's patience finally snapped, and he tried to stab his rival. Ramin threw him to the ground and escaped, but was borne down by guilt at the terrible offence he had committed against the royal dignity. On the advice of a counsellor who came to speak with him the following morning, he made up his mind to leave Marv and try to forget Vis. Mubad encouraged him in his plan by granting him the governorship of a distant western province.

A 19th-century mural of holy Muslim women dressed in long veils. In the story of Vis and Ramin, Ramin, disguised in a woman's long veil, managed to gain entry to the palace where Vis was living. But it was not as easy to win back her love.

There, Ramin found a new love, a Parthian princess named Gul whom he married. Yet the old flame was revived by a series of ten letters from Vis. And when he was offered a nosegay of violets, recalling one that Vis had once given him, saying "Keep this always in remembrance of me", he determined to return to Marv.

When he first arrived, Vis was angry at his infidelity and refused to see him. Only when, days later, he rode away broken-hearted did she finally relent and agree to become reconciled. The two again became lovers.

Unsuspecting, Mubad welcomed his brother back from the west but, no doubt sensing the danger of a rapprochement with Vis, soon after insisted he accompany him on a hunting expedition. The prospect of separation so soon after their reunion proved altogether too much for the lovers, and they finally decided on desperate measures.

Ramin set out with Mubad but soon after sneaked back to Marv under cover of night. Dressed in a woman's long veil, he managed to gain entrance to the king's palace. There he and his men attacked the royal garrison, killing them all including his own half-brother Zard. Then he and Vis plundered the royal treasury and rode away to start a new life in the west.

According to Zoroastrian tradition the dead cannot be buried for fear of soiling the purity of the earth. Corpses were, instead, left on top of Towers of Silence, like these in Yazd, central Iran.

When Mubad heard of their defection, his world fell about his ears. For a week he would talk to no one; then he announced that he would seek the fugitives with his army. But fate was not on his side. As the troops halted for the night, a wild boar broke into the camp. The king leaped onto his horse to confront it but the beast charged, bringing down the horse and goring the king fatally.

And so, unexpectedly, Ramin found himself ruler of Marv. He mounted the throne with Vis by his side. They reigned jointly and justly for many decades, during which the only three things in short supply in their kingdom, Gurgani claimed, were trouble, pain and grief.

When Vis finally died, leaving her husband two children, the grieving Ramin built a Tower of Silence to receive her body. Then he abdicated the throne to his eldest son, and spent his declining days by the tower. There he died and his remains were laid to rest beside those of the woman he loved. Their souls were united, the poet concluded, and "in heaven those two constant spirits were once more joined as bride and groom".

127

How Chess Came to Persia

According to a legend recounted by the poet Firdowsi, the game of chess came to Persia in the form of an intellectual challenge posed by an Indian emperor. With its infinity of permutations, chess soon became a favourite pastime at the Persian court.

In the reign of the illustrious Khusrow I, known to his subjects as Anushirvan ("He of the Immortal Soul"), an embassy came to the Persian court from an emperor of India's mighty Gupta dynasty. The spectacle was magnificent in the extreme, as befitted the grandeur of both the sender and the recipient. There were elephants carrying *howdahs*, splendidly caparisoned horsemen and no fewer than 1,000 camels laden with gifts that included musk, amber, aloes-wood, damascened scimitars, richly decorated jewel-boxes and sunshades cunningly worked with costly gem-stones and gold.

Yet the gift saved for last was none of these things. It was a flat board marked out in squares, and the Persian emperor had never seen anything quite like it before. Accompanying it were a number of small figures carved from ivory or teak. Intrigued, the ruler waited for the envoy to explain their use. But no exposition was forthcoming. Instead the Indian issued a challenge – one of a playful kind, yet with a message of real political import.

"May you live as long as the heavens endure!" he began grandiloquently, but what he went on to communicate was rather less deferential. His master, the Indian emperor, wished the Persian ruler to summon all the finest minds of his kingdom to see if they could work out the rules of the game he saw before him. If they could establish the parts

Elephants carried the gift of chess to Persia from India and later the animals became pieces in the game. This glazed elephant with *howdah* and riders dates from the 13th century.

played by the various pieces and the moves each one made, his master would gladly forward the tribute the Persian ruler traditionally demanded. If not, however, he would expect to receive tribute in return, for, as the envoy tactfully put it, "science is superior to any wealth".

Khusrow considered the Indian's words long and carefully. He questioned him about the nature of the game, and learned that it mimicked warfare and that its tactics and strategy were those of the battlefield. Eventually the king decided to accept the challenge. He told the envoy he would need eight days to solve the problem, after which he would communicate the answer and expect the regular tribute.

The emissary took his leave, and Khusrow at once summoned all his wisest counsellors. They studied the game intently and made many suggestions, but none came close to mastering its mysteries. Then at last the king turned to his most brilliant adviser, Bozorgmeihr. This man had first won the king's favour as a student, when he had interpreted a dream that had much troubled the monarch; since then he had become a permanent fixture at court, encouraging learning, studying the secrets of the stars and surpassing all men in the practice of physic.

Now he focused the full force of his finely tuned intellect on the problem at hand, studying the board and the pieces on it for a full day and night. At the end of that time, he instructed the shah to summon the envoy, and to the Indian's amazement proceeded to expound the game of chess in every detail.

The Gaming-Table Turned

His ingenuity did not end there. As Firdowsi tells the tale, he went on to turn the tables on the Indian emperor by inventing the game of *nard* or backgammon – and offering the same challenge in reverse. The spiked board and counters were sent off ceremonially to the Gupta court along with 2,000 camel-loads of treasure, with the proviso that if the nation's Brahmin intellectuals failed to fathom the mysteries of this new puzzle, the Persians would expect double the amount of treasure in return. Bozorgmeihr won the bet, and the emperor sent Khusrow a full year's tribute.

Although the poet no doubt embroidered the story, his account of chess's arrival in Persia seems to have had at least some basis in fact. Chess is indeed thought to have reached the country in Khusrow I's reign, and it did come from India, where it had apparently evolved from a game known as *chaturanga* (in Persian, *shatranj*). As described by the poet, the game Bozorgmeihr puzzled over seems to have had some features of this earlier one, being played on a board of 100 squares rather than the sixty-four familiar today.

In place of the queen was a piece representing a royal counsellor, who always had to remain on a square adjacent to his king. Pieces representing horses took the part of the knight, while turrets closely approximated the present-day castle. Elephants stood in for the bishops, and the other two spaces in the back rows were occupied by camels, whose three-square trajectories apparently resembled the knight's move familiar today.

In other respects the game was remarkably similar to that played nowadays. When a player brought an opponent's king under attack he was expected to say out loud, "King, beware!" in much the same way as a modern player would say "Check". The opposing player then had to move the challenged piece to a square where it was no longer threatened.

As for the checkmate situation, Firdowsi described it in elegant terms befitting a poet: "Looking around in all directions, the king sees the enemy encircling him. Water and trenches block his path; there are hostile troops on all sides. Exhausted and thirsty, the monarch can do nothing; that is the fate decreed for him by the ever-changing sky."

Chess began life in India as the tactical wargame *chaturanga* and was already popular by the 2nd century AD. According to the myth it came to Persia during the rule of Khusrow I. This undated image is from an illuminated Persian treatise on chess.

Love Lost and Found

The real-life love affair between Khusrow Parviz, the last great Sasanian ruler, and his Christian wife Shirin inspired poets of later generations to create the romantic legend of a king thwarted in love and ambition.

Khusrow II Parviz ("the Victorious") and Shirin were both historical figures. Khusrow II, who ruled Persia from AD590 to 628, was the last great conqueror of the pre-Islamic era. Shirin too was a real person, and the chronicles vouch for the special place she occupied in Khusrow's life.

Shirin was a Christian, born into a noble family. The marriage may initially have been designed to win the support of the nation's Christian community, but it quickly turned into a love match. The two were together for thirty years, and Shirin was by her husband's side when he was eventually slain, faithful to the last.

Great Persian poets were to embroider these hard facts into a tragic love story. The first to address the subject was Firdowsi in the *Shahnameh*. In his panoramic view of Persian history, Khusrow was a flawed monarch who paved the way for national defeat. He grew up to be a mighty warrior and a flamboyant sovereign, yet in Firdowsi's telling he was not a good ruler. He imposed new taxes on the people and chose as his advisors traitors who were in league with his enemies.

Shirin, too, was at best an ambiguous heroine for Firdowsi. He claimed she poisoned her principal rival to assure herself of Khusrow's love. Her big scene in the *Shahnameh* comes after her husband's death, when she wins over Khusrow's son

The story of Khusrow and Shirin was a favourite one for Persian artists. But while paintings, like this one from Shiraz, c.16th century, remained sumptuous representations of courtly love, written versions were not always so generous to the lovers.

The Conjuror of Courtly Love

The epic romance of Khusrow and Shirin was one of five penned by Nizami of Ganja, the greatest of Persia's poets of courtly love.

Nizami (left, centre) discourses with attendants. Book cover, Qajar, 1867.

Nizami had an uneventful life. Although he was born in Iran he spent most of his life in Ganja in the Caucasus area of what is now Azerbaijan. He was orphaned at an early age, and only once left Ganja to meet the ruling prince.

Today he is remembered as the author of the *Khamseh*, a quintet of short epics written in rhyming couplets. "Khusrow and Shirin" is one of three devoted to celebrated love stories; the other two tell of Majnun who went mad for the love of Leyla, and the Seven Beauties pursued by the Sasanian ruler Bahram V, also known as Bahram Gur.

Nizami's twelfth-century work was popular throughout Persian society and set a fashion for similar sequences by other poets

writing in both Persian and Turkish. In later centuries it also proved an inspiration for

countless artists, providing the subject-matter for many dramatic paintings.

Shiruy, the historical Kavad II, and then, when the new ruler asks her to marry him, chooses instead to die by her own hand in her husband's tomb.

Firdowsi's treatment seemed dry and grudging to Nizami of Ganja, writing 150 years after. The later poet saw the story simply as a great romance of thwarted love. Historically, his version has little real about it other than the names of the principal characters; but as a tale of tragic passion it has survived the centuries unscathed.

Nizami's Khusrow is handsome, wise, brave and strong. As a young man he dreams that his grandfather, Khusrow I, predicts his future: he will meet the love of his life, find the swiftest horse in the land, patronize a minstrel whose words could sweeten even poison, and inherit a throne.

All the old king's predictions come true. The minstrel is Barbad, father of Persian music; the throne is that of Persia. And he encounters the girl and the horse in a lakeside scene that became a favourite subject for painters in later centuries.

At the time, both Khusrow and Shirin had already fallen in love, simply by report. The go-between was the prince's friend Shapur, who first roused Khusrow's passion with glowing accounts of the beauty of Shirin, daughter of the queen of Armenia, and then travelled to that land to show her Khusrow's portrait, which produced a similar effect. Taking from her mother's stables the horse Shabdiz, the one foreseen in Khusrow's dream, the princess fled the court for the Sasanian capital of Ctesiphon, hoping to meet her love.

131

Khusrow and the Fisherman

An anecdote from the **Thousand and One Nights** *told how a poor fisherman used his wits to benefit from Khusrow's fabled generosity and drew the ire of his quarrelsome wife.*

The fisherman brought a huge fish he had caught to the palace and, as he had hoped, Khusrow gave him the vast sum of 4,000 drachm for it. Shocked by such largesse, Queen Shirin objected that it was too much since their courtiers would complain if they were paid less than a fisherman for their services. Khusrow saw her point, but insisted that a king could not go back on his word, so Shirin urged him to reject the fish outright. "Ask the man if it's male or female," she suggested. "If he says 'male', say you wanted a female, and if he says 'female', say 'We want a male'."

Khusrow recalled his visitor and put the question, but the fisherman judiciously replied "It is neither male nor female." The monarch laughed, and ordered that he should have another 4,000 drachm for his astuteness.

As the fisherman was leaving the hall, he dropped one of the coins and fell to his knees to pick it up. "See?" said Shirin. "With all that money, he's still too greedy to leave a single coin behind." So the king called him back to reprimand him. But the fisherman replied that he was only worried that someone might stand on the coin, which bore the king's likeness, and so offend the royal dignity. Delighted by the reply, the king

gave him a third bag of coins and then jokingly advised his courtiers to beware of taking their wives' advice lest it end up costing them three times what they originally intended to pay.

At the same time Khusrow was travelling north to find her. Their paths crossed at a wayside lake where Shirin had stopped to bathe. The two saw one another and were stricken, but each failed to recognize the other's true identity. There were to be many further setbacks before the lovers finally met, by which time Khusrow had inherited the Persian throne and was struggling to defend it from the ambitions of a rival, Bahram Chubin.

Even when the couple did finally come together, their troubles were far from over. Ardently the young king declared his passion. But Shirin had been warned by her mother not to give in too easily, so she tactfully rejected his advances.

Used always to getting his way, the headstrong suitor rode off in a fury on Shabdiz towards the Byzantine capital of Constantinople, where he took his revenge by agreeing to marry Maryam, the daughter of the emperor. (In this detail Nizami was respecting history, for Khusrow did once seal a marriage alliance with Byzantium, hoping to cement peace between the two powers.) By this impulsive action, he sowed the seeds of future tragedy but gained immediate political advantage. With the support of the Byzantine army, he was able to defeat Bahram and return in triumph to Ctesiphon as undisputed ruler of Persia.

Meanwhile Shirin became queen of Armenia following the death of her mother. And in time she too found a new lover. His name was Farhad, a mighty stonemason, famed for his great strength.

On learning that he had a rival, Khusrow's jealousy was stirred and his passion revived. First he tried to buy off Farhad with gold, but when that attempt failed he sought to distance him from the queen by giving him a seemingly impossible task: to cut a pass through the mountain of Bisitun on the ancient road from Ecbatana to Babylon.

Sasanian coin from the reign of Khusrow II, AD590–628, bearing the monarch's head.

Farhad accepted, on condition that Khusrow give up all claims to Shirin's affections if he succeeded. Then he set to work.

One day Shirin chose to visit him at the site, donning all her jewellery to impress her lover. The burden of the gems was too much for her horse, which sank to the ground beneath their weight. But Farhad quickly came to the rescue. Raising horse, rider and jewels on his shoulders, he carried his magnificent load all the way back to Shirin's palace – a display of strength unequalled even in his prodigious record.

Hearing of Farhad's feat and learning too that he was likely to complete the assignment, Khusrow realized that he risked losing Shirin for ever. Faced with that terrible prospect, he resorted to deceit, sending a message to the mason falsely stating that Shirin was dead. It had the effect he had envisaged: despairing, Farhad flung himself from the mountain to his death.

Khusrow's wife Maryam died soon after, but still he and his true love remained separated. In Nizami's telling, it was finally music that brought them together. Two court minstrels, Nakiseh and Barbad, sang a duet in which Nakiseh took Shirin's part and Barbad expressed all Khusrow's pent-up passion. The plaintive strains melted the lovers' hearts. And at last they agreed to marry.

But there was no happy ending. In a final, ironic twist of fate, Shiruy, Khusrow's son by Maryam, fell in love with Shirin at the nuptials. Consumed by jealousy, he treacherously stabbed Khusrow to death as he slept beside his bride.

This final loss was too much for Shirin to bear. On the day of her husband's funeral she locked herself in his tomb and took her own life. When her body was found, she was ceremonially laid to rest with the king. The couple so long separated in life finally came together in death.

THE PERSIAN LEGACY

Over the centuries since Cyrus the Great first formed the Persian empire, the country has undergone countless incarnations. Ancient Persia itself disappeared with the Islamic conquest in the years after AD633, and periods of occupation by Mongols, Turks and even Europeans have brought the influence of a great many cultures. But even today, with the days of monarchy over, traces of Persia's ancient past live on.

With the seventh-century Arab invasion, the country lost not only its independence but also its religion and even its language, for by the end of the century the Pahlavi or Middle Persian tongue spoken under the Sasanians had been replaced in official dealings by Arabic. In time the new language gained in popularity for its own virtues – it was richer and more adaptable than Middle Persian, as well as used over a wider geographical area – and when the native tongue was reborn as New Persian from the ninth century on, it borrowed much from the idiom of the conquerors. In religious affairs, the new rulers, in theory at least, practised tolerance, though they did so with the

Zoroastrians take part in a fire-lighting ceremony, in modern-day Tehran. Although it was supplanted as the state religion more than 1,000 years ago, the religion still survives in Iran today.

forbearance of people certain that they brought with them the true faith. In practice, that meant that they did not proscribe Zoroastrianism, but they did discriminate against its practitioners. As it became clear that adherence to Islam was a necessary precondition for thriving under the new dispensation, voluntary conversions became widespread. It took a century or more for Islam to embed itself firmly in the national consciousness, but in the end its triumph was almost complete.

Even so, pockets of the old faith survived, first in the east of the country, far from the centres of Arab power, and then in southern Iran. The remaining believers were dismissively called *gabr*, a word related to the term for "infidel". They were obliged to wear distinctive clothing and pay a special tax, as well as being forbidden to ride horses or bear arms. Even so, they held out, and a Zoroastrian community exists in Iran to this day.

One of the reasons for their long endurance has been the existence of a flourishing Zoroastrian colony in India far away to the south. Known even now as Parsis or Persians, its members trace their descent from people who left Iran to escape persecution in the ninth to tenth centuries, 200 years after the coming of Islam. In India they settled first in Goa and then principally in Bombay, where over the centuries they grew rich as merchants and traders. Although they lost contact for a long time with their co-religionists to the north, communication was re-established in the fifteenth century, and in later times they did much to try to better the condition of the surviving Persian Zoroastrians.

The Iranian Zoroastrians and the Parsis remain the chief link with the ancient Persian faith. In recent years their numbers have been declining, partly as a result of immigration to the West and increased contact with non-Zoroastrians. The celebrated Towers of Silence, where Zoroastrians have traditionally left their dead so as not to defile the sacred elements of earth, fire or water, are gradually falling into disuse. Even so, there are now substantial Zoroastrian communities in Britain, Canada, the USA and Australia, and their traditions show no signs of dying out.

A story-teller recounts the tale of Sohrab and Rustam with the help of an illustrated backdrop. This tradition is one of the oldest in Iran and has survived the coming of film and television.

The Fortunes of Firdowsi's Heroes

The secular inheritance of ancient Persia also had chequered fortunes in the centuries following the coming of Islam. Stories from Firdowsi's *Shahnameh* were – and to an extent still are – recounted in towns and villages across the country by professional story-tellers known as *naqqal* (see page 111). As a result, illiterate villagers grew up with the heroes of the saga very much part of their lives, and even today an awareness of the deeds of Rustam, Sohrab, Isfandiyar and the like are part of every Iranian's heritage.

Yet for a work that occupies such a central part in its own nation's literary tradition, the *Shahnameh* has not travelled well. Translations into the main European languages were made in the nineteenth century, but for the most part they failed to attract much attention, perhaps because foreign readers were discouraged by the book's resolutely nationalistic tone. One of the few non-Persian works to have been directly inspired by it

With their mix of intrigue and exoticism, Persian tales proved irresistible to Hollywood. This scene is from Universal's 1942 production of *The Arabian Nights*, starring Mary Montese.

In the wake of the revolution of 1979 the *Shahnameh* was banned for a few years, but this failed to dampen the public's appetite for the poem, by now a vital part of Iranian national identity. Other channels for these deeply charged historical passions are provided by the passion plays that are a distinctive part of the national culture. The best-known of these dramas, performed by all-male casts in mosques and bazaars as well as in purpose-built theatres known as *takiyeh*, recount the martyrdom of Imam Husayn, the grandson of the prophet Mohammed whose death opened up the schism between Shi'ite and Sunni Muslims. But players also sometimes enact the death of Siyavush (see page 84), one of the heroes of the *Shahnameh*, following an even older secular tradition dating back at least to Firdowsi's time.

was *Sohrab and Rustam*, by the Victorian poet Matthew Arnold; a moving work in Homeric vein, it takes as its theme Firdowsi's story of the killing of the hero Sohrab in single combat by his own father, who is unaware of his opponent's true identity (see page 83). Yet even Arnold had little direct knowledge of his source; he read of the story in the writings of the French critic Charles Augustin Sainte-Beuve, and never read more than a few paragraphs of Firdowsi in translation.

The *Shahnameh* is still read avidly in Iran, although in recent times it has had its detractors. During the 1960s and 1970s, its enduring popularity led a small group of left-wing Iranian intellectuals to dismiss the poem, vaunting instead the works of less crowd-pleasing poets. But outright hostility to the work was more often shaped by a political antipathy to the late Shah of Iran, Mohammed Reza Pahlavi. By building the Azadi Monument in Tehran in 1971 to mark the 2,500th anniversary of the Persian empire and staging a sumptuous state dinner at Persepolis in 1971, the Shah sought to associate himself with the deeds of the Achaemenian kings – and for those who were disenchanted with his rule, such grand gestures offered a symbolic focus.

From Word of Mouth to Silver Screen

If the heroic legends are best remembered within Iran's borders, the racier, more down-to-earth tales that found their way into the *Thousand and One Nights* have gone around the world. The stories Shehrezad told to put off her own execution have delighted generations of readers in all the major languages. In bowdlerized versions, they have also provided the plots for well-loved children's entertainments and pantomimes, and most recently given the Disney Corporation a worldwide hit in the feature-length animation *Aladdin*.

The *Thousand and One Nights* was first introduced to a Western audience at the start of the eighteenth century by a French linguist and traveller named Antoine Galland. Inspired by the success of a translation of the Sinbad stories that he had brought out in 1701, he went on to publish twelve further volumes over the next fourteen years. In doing so, he helped to give definitive form to the work, for no complete Arabic manuscript predating his translation has survived; indeed, no earlier versions of some of the best-known stories, featuring Aladdin and Ali Baba, have yet been found, leading some critics to suggest that he might have made them up himself.

What is certain is that the work was an instant success, and not just in France. Chapbooks pirated from Galland soon started appearing across the Channel. More than a century was to pass before the great scholarly English interpretations of the Arabists E.W. Lane and Sir Richard Burton, but long before their time tales of Shehrezad and Aladdin and Sinbad the Sailor had already become part of the popular tradition. They even spawned a passing European fashion for things Persian, stimulated by the same taste for Oriental exoticism that was to inspire the eighteenth-century vogue for chinoiserie. One of its earliest monuments was Montesquieu's *Lettres Persanes*, which used the device of a correspondence between two fictional Persian noblemen to take a satirical look at the state of contemporary France. Almost a century later, James Morier had success in England with his picaresque novel *Hajji Baba of Isfahan*, which drew on his experiences as a diplomat in Persia.

The vogue for Persian exoticism soon faded, but the influence of the narrative techniques employed in the *Thousand and One Nights* was to prove more enduring. In particular, the tale-within-a-tale was to strike a lasting chord with Western writers. The extraordinary Polish adventurer and scholar Count Jan Potocki built his cult Gothic fiction *The Saragossa Manuscript* entirely around the device, which was also also explored by the likes of George Meredith and Robert Louis Stevenson. The best-known twentieth-century exponent of the art is the Argentinian writer Jorge Luis Borges, who has retold certain of the original tales.

Sadly, the worldwide success of the *Thousand and One Nights* has been the exception rather than the rule for Persian culture generally. Judged on a global scale, it is hard to think of any other tradition of such antiquity and literary richness that is less well known around the world. Part of the problem is political; the Iranian Revolution effectively cut the nation off from the West just at the time when barriers to international communication were elsewhere coming down. Yet much can be put down to sheer unfamiliarity. For most people outside the country, Persian mythology is simply an unknown; but in an increasingly interconnected world, even the best-kept secrets have a way of getting out.

Giant murals appeared throughout Iran during the Iran–Iraq war of the 1980s. Their heroic imagery served an inspirational purpose similar to the rock-reliefs of the ancient Persians.

Glossary

apadana A pillared audience hall built by Darius I at Susa and Persepolis. It was able to accommodate 10,000 supplicants to the King of Kings.

asha Truth, one of the cornerstones of Zorostrianism, which is built on the tension between the opposites of *asha* and *druj*, the lie.

ashavan The righteous followers of the Good Religion who have been shown the correct path by the Holy Immortals.

chaturanga The forerunner of chess, played on 100 squares, which came to Persia from India during Khusrow I's reign. The modern game uses sixty-four squares.

daeva A false god. The ancient term from which the Persian *div* derives.

div The demons who made up Angra Mainyu's army of evil spirits.

druj The lie, the opposite of *asha* or truth. The dualism of these two concepts underscored all Zoroastrian belief. This word is sometimes used to describe Angra Mainyu's demon army.

farr The divine and kingly glory that passed down from monarch to monarch through the Iranian royal line.

fravashi The celestial souls of people who elected to help Ahura Mazda in the protracted battle against evil.

getig The physical part of the universe. When Ahura Mazda created the world, he oversaw two parts: the immaterial universe, or *menog*, and its physical counterpart, *getig*.

hamestagan Also known as Misvan Gatu, or "Place of the Mixed Ones", in Zoroastrian cosmology, describing the destination of souls for whom the scales of judgement are balanced, having led lives neither wholly bad nor purely good.

haoma The powerful intoxicant drunk by Persian priests who wish to commune with the gods in ancient rituals.

howdah The often elaborate platforms which provided seating for those travelling by elephant.

jinn Powerful spirits also known as genies.

khuniyagar Minstrels who were important and respected figures at court. Competition for such posts was fierce, as shown by the story of Barbad.

naqqal The professional story-tellers who, even today, travel around Iran recounting tales from the great Persian epics. They remain the oldest living link to Persia's ancient cultural past.

pairaka Dangerously seductive female demons who are often characterized in the animal kingdom as bright-eyed rats.

pardehdar Travelling story-tellers who used illustrated backdrops and props to dramatize the tales they told.

peri Derived from the *pairaka* of the *Avesta*, these beautiful female spirits became, much later, beneficial presences formed from fire. They became, for the Western world, the fairies of folklore.

yazata "Worshipful Ones" of Zoroastrianism who were created by the Holy Immortals as warriors against evil. They are believed to be derived from the pagan gods of the ancient Iranians.

Index

Page numbers in *italic* denote captions. Where there is a textual reference to the topic on the same page as a caption, italics have not been used.

143

Further Reading

Amiet, Pierre. *Elam*. Paris, 1966.
Amiet, Pierre. *Suse 6000 ans d'histoire*. Louvre Museum: Paris, 1988.
Canby, Sheila R. *Persian Painting*. British Museum Press: London, 1993.
Curtis, John. *Ancient Persia*. British Museum Press: London, 1996.
Curtis, Vesta Sarkhosh. *Persian Myths*. British Museum Press: London, 1997.
Ferrier, Ronald. *The Arts of Persia*. London, 1989.
Hinnells, John R. *Persian Mythology*. Peter Bedrick Books: New York, 1985.
Hinz, Walter. *Das Reich Elam*. Stuttgart, 1964.
Irving, Clive. *Crossroads of Civilization*. Weidenfeld & Nicolson: London, 1979.
Levy, Reuben. *The Epic of the Kings*. Routledge & Kegan Paul: London, 1967.
Picard, Barbara Leonie. *Tales of Ancient Persia*. OUP: Oxford, 1993.
Roaf, Michael. *Cultural Atlas of Mesopotamia and the Ancient Near East*. Oxford, 1990.
Wiesehofer, Josef. *Ancient Persia*. IB Tauris: London, 1996.

Picture Credits

The publisher would like to thank the following people, museums and photographic libraries for permission to reproduce their material. Every care has been taken to trace copyright holders. However, if we have omitted anyone we apologize and will, if informed, make corrections in any future edition.

Key:
t top; **c** centre; **b** bottom; **l** left; **r** right

Abbreviations:

BAL	Bridgeman Art Library, London/New York
BM	British Museum, London
Christie's	Christie's Images, London
ET	e.t. archive, London
RHPL	Robert Harding Picture Library
V&A	Victoria & Albert Museum, London
WFA	Werner Forman Archive, London

Cover: Louvre, Paris/BAL; **title page** BAL/BL; **contents page** BM; **6** ET; **7** Christie's; **8** Ashmolean Museum, Oxford/BAL; **10** Ashmolean Museum, Oxford/BAL; **11** BAL; **12** Louvre/BAL; **13** British Museum/Michael Holford; **14l** Louvre/ET; **14r** Ashmolean Museum, Oxford; **15l** Schimmel Collection, New York/WFA; **15r** Adam Woolfit/RHPL; **16** Louvre/BAL; **17** V&A/ET; **18–19** ET; **20** RHPL; **21** Royal Asiatic Society/BAL; **22t** BM/ET; **22l** RHPL; **22r** Vesta Curtis; **23t** RHPL; **23b** RHPL; **24tl** ET; **24tr** RHPL; **25l** ET; **25r** Louvre/BAL; **26** Christie's; **27** Bodleian Library, Oxford; **28** RHPL; **29** BAL; **30** BM (1906.11.3.2366); **31** BM (WA123267); **34** BM (1843-6-20) **35** Christie's; **36** BM (OA1943.10-9.02); **37** BAL; **39** Christie's; **40** V&A (IS3393-1883/CT7588); **41** Christie's; **42** British Library (OR371 f.17r); **43** Chester Beatty Library of Oriental Art/BAL; **44** Hutchison Library; **45** BAL; **47** BAL; **48l** Georg Gerster/Network; **48r** RHPL; **49t** Bibliotheque National, Paris/BAL; **49b** Christie's; **50** BM (OA1948.10-9.053); **51** RHPL; **54** BM (CM1850-4-12-90); **55** RHPL; **56** V&A/BAL; **57** BM (WA132256.123/OT8); **58** BM (WA123901/OT1); **59** Louvre/BAL; **60** BM (OA1930.4-12.02); **61** RHPL; **62** Metropolitan Museum, New York/WFA; **63** BM (WA119985); **64** Christie's; **65** Louvre/BAL; **68** BM (WA124092); **69** BM (OA1920.9-17.0275); **70–71t** Louvre/BAL; **70–71b** Isabella Tree/Hutchison; **71** Christie's; **72** RHPL; **73** BM/BAL; **74** Royal Asiatic Society; **75** Christie's; **76** British Library (OR 8761 f.52v); **77** BM (WA123910); **79** National Museum of India, Delhi/BAL; **80** Christie's; **81** Christie's; **82** BM (WA124000); **83** BM (OA1922.7-11.02); **84–85** BM (OA 1948.12-11.027-8); **86** Christie's; **87** Christie's; **88** BM (OA 1975.5-23.04); **89** RHPL; **90–91** RHPL; **93** Louvre/BAL; **94** BM (WA124081); **95** Bonhams/BAL; **96–97** Christie's; **98** BM (OA1948.10-9.052); **99** V&A (IS3378/CT47859); **100** BM (OA1948.12-11.025); **102** Fogg Art Museum at Harvard University, USA; **103** BM (1919-8-20-1); **105** BM (WA90920); **107** RHPL; **108l** BM (124095); **108r** Christie's; **109t** BL (Or 371 folio 35); **109b** BM (WAA 135913); **110** V&A/BAL; **111** V&A Museum, London (442-1884/CT290); **112** BM (OA1974.6.17 10 (13)); **113** Bibliotheque Nationale, Paris/BAL; **114** V&A (IS294-1951/CT22641); **115** Christie's; **117** Christie's/BAL; **118** V&A (IS133-1964/CT8835); **119** National Museum of India, Delhi/BAL; **120** BAL; **121** Christie's; **122** BM (WA123906/OT9); **123** British Library/Michael Holford; **124** British Library/BAL; **126** Iman Zahdah Chah Zaid Mosque, Isfahan, Iran/BAL; **127** RHPL; **128** Christie's; **129** Royal Asiatic Society/BAL; **130** Christie's; **131** Christie's/BAL; **133** Michael Holford; **134** Frank Spooner Agency; **135** Michael Wood; **136** Kobal Collection; **137** Frank Spooner Agency.